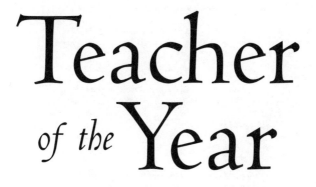

Teacher of the Year

More Than 400 Quotes of Insight,

Inspiration, and Motivation from

America's Greatest Teachers

Frank Sennett

Contemporary Books

Chicago   New York   San Francisco   Lisbon   London   Madrid   Mexico City
Milan   New Delhi   San Juan   Seoul   Singapore   Sydney   Toronto

Library of Congress Cataloging-in-Publication Data

Teacher of the year : more than 400 quotes of insight, inspiration, and
motivation from America's greatest teachers / [compiled by] Frank Sennett.
     p.   cm.
   Includes index.
   ISBN 0-07-140990-4
   1. Education—Quotations, maxims, etc.   2. Teaching—Quotations,
maxims, etc.   3. Teachers—United States—Quotations.   I. Sennett, Frank.

PN6084.E38 T427   2003
371.102—dc21   2002071256

*I wish to acknowledge and thank three teachers who had a profound impact on
my development as a writer: Wayne Seitz, Dick Schwarzlose, and Bill Kittredge.*

*This book is for the members of my family who have served as educators,
teaching everything from Sunday school and Red Cross life-saving courses to
grade-school and university classes: Clint & Muriel, Frank Sr., Mary Lou, Emma,
Leslie, Michael, Marsha, Pete, and Amy.*

*It is also dedicated to Cal, who taught me the finer points of baseball, business,
and being a man of integrity.*

1 2 3 4 5 6 7 8 9 0   LBM/LBM   1 0 9 8 7 6 5 4 3 2

ISBN 0-07-140990-4

McGraw-Hill books are available at special quantity discounts to use as premiums
and sales promotions, or for use in corporate training programs. For more
information, please write to the Director of Special Sales, Professional Publishing,
McGraw-Hill, Two Penn Plaza, New York, NY 10121-2298. Or contact your local
bookstore.

This book is printed on acid-free paper.

Contents

Preface

Upon being named Teacher of the Year for Norman, Oklahoma, LuAnne Lasley exclaimed, "I feel like Julia Roberts without the money and the dress!"

And when Judith Moore was honored as Teacher of the Year in Polk County, Florida, she told assembled well-wishers, "I feel like Sandra Bullock in *Miss Congeniality*."

While they don't enjoy the glamour and wealth of Hollywood idols, teachers can count themselves among society's true heroes. After all, they help us unwrap the priceless gift of learning.

Even bigger-than-life celebrities understand the paramount role educators play in our lives. When National Teacher of the Year Philip Bigler was asked to describe the most exciting moment of his tenure, he cited his appearance on "The Late Show with David Letterman."

"It was a real validation of our profession, and Dave couldn't have been nicer," Bigler said. "After I completed my interview and had actually left the stage, Letterman told Paul Shaffer, the band director, on the air, 'Wouldn't it be nice to know that when you went to work every day, you were making a tangible difference in the future of the world?' That was a wonderful tribute to teachers everywhere."

The following pages showcase the wit and wisdom of top teachers from all fifty states and the District of Columbia—including twenty-two who earned the title National Teacher of the Year. These honored few speak for the thousands of dedicated instructors who feed the nation's hungry young minds every day. As Normal, Illinois, Teacher of the Year Mary Ellen Somers so aptly put it, "All teachers who commit to their classrooms are teachers of the year."

Clearly, we should shine the spotlight on educators every chance we get.

It's More Than a Job

Teaching as a Calling

Teaching is a calling, not a career move.

> —BRUCE M. PENNIMAN,
> *Massachusetts Teacher of the Year*

I remember the excitement of my first year teaching. The smell of the chalk, my own desk and mailbox. I planned all summer; reading, asking questions, visiting classrooms, and making paper cutouts of the desks and kidney-shaped tables so I could set up the perfect classroom.

> —TERRI K. FISHBOUGH,
> *Tulare County, California, Teacher of the Year*

I see teaching as a service to humanity, basically. It's always been important for me to put back what I take out.

> —DON JOHNSON, *Minnesota Teacher of the Year*

Teaching is leaving a legacy to the planet. Teaching, to me, touches eternity.

> —JACKIE PARKER, *Mississippi Teacher of the Year*

I share the excitement of work with other teachers and my students, and their enthusiasm and sense of possibility increases. And we will never truly know how many students' lives are changed by our sense of responsibility and the excitement that we have toward living.

> —*California's* MARILYN JACHETTI WHIRRY,
> *National Teacher of the Year*

Teaching is the focal point of my universe. I'm at peace in the classroom. I'm called to teach just as any priest or nun. Aside from family, it's the most sacred part of my existence. I can't conceive of ever leaving the classroom entirely. Very few people are lucky to find where they are supposed to be in life. There are a lot of wanderers out there. I was lucky to find it.

> —RICHARD CHAPLEAU,
> *California Teacher of the Year*

In my teaching, I celebrate on a daily basis the joy of learning.

> —CHARLES ZEZULKA,
> *Connecticut Teacher of the Year*

Scientists get rewards when they discover things. The kind of rewards I get are when I've reached a child or when I've helped them understand. There can be nothing more rewarding than that.

—DONNA FISHER,
    Rockwall, Texas, Secondary Teacher of the Year

It's a fantastic feeling to transmit something you know. I was so hungry for education myself that I feel now that I don't want any children to remain hungry.

—*New York's* JAY SOMMER,
    National Teacher of the Year

I work in a profession that I feel has been truly blessed. What other profession offers a person an opportunity to touch so many lives?

—FRED H. GOWER, *New Jersey Teacher of the Year*

This isn't a job for me. This is life.

—MARY CAFFEY, *Nebraska Teacher of the Year*

I was born to be a teacher. It's all I've ever wanted to do. When I was a child, my mother gave me a memory book, and every year I wrote in it that I wanted to become a teacher. Being a teacher is one of the most influential professions in the world. We are training the future leaders, doctors, engineers, and scientists. We need to be proud of the fact that we're teachers.

—AMY MONROE DENTY,
Georgia Teacher of the Year

I've always felt a tug toward education. I like doing everything I can to ensure the success of the children.

—FAITH KLINE, *Pennsylvania Teacher of the Year*

Teachers must be celebrated for moving civilization from ignorance to enlightenment, from apathy to responsibility.

—*Ohio's* SHARON M. DRAPER,
National Teacher of the Year

The classroom teacher is what education is all about. Try to run a school without teachers.

—JANICE FITZSIMMONS,
New Jersey Teacher of the Year

A lot of people believe that with the focus on technology, distance learning will replace teachers in the classroom. But I think you will always need the human touch in the classroom.

> —MARTHA KORIOTH, *Elementary Teacher of the Year for Texas's Irving Independent School District*

As a child, I was taught that being helpful is a privilege, because not everybody is in a position to give help, or is asked to give help.

> —MARJORIE DRAHOS, *New Jersey Teacher of the Year*

There are certain exciting moments in teaching, and I don't know if they are able to be experienced anywhere else.

> —MARK WRIGHT, *Teacher of the Year for Bergen County, New Jersey*

There are some things that a classroom teacher can do that just nobody else can, I don't care how much authority they have.

> —ANNIE PEGRAM, *North Carolina Teacher of the Year*

Teaching is serving. It's ministering to kids, parents, the community, everybody.

—PIEDAD YMBERT, *Texas Teacher of the Year*

Without teachers, there would be no other profession.

—JULIA KOBLE, *North Dakota Teacher of the Year*

People will always forget what you do, and they will always forget what you say, but they will never, ever forget the way you make them feel.

—AMELIA STANELLE,
Teacher of the Year at Muscogee County, Ohio's Blackmon Road Middle School

If we give back to the community where we live, we are always educating the future generations by being role models, and inspiring everyone around us—the people we serve as well as the little ones coming behind us. And it feels good to make a difference in other people's lives.

—ANITA LYONS, *Texas English as Second Language Teacher of the Year*

Every day, we touch the lives of so many people.

> —NICHOLAS J. ULIANO,
> *Pennsylvania Teacher of the Year*

In high school, I was never a beauty queen or could play sports, and I always wondered, "What can I do? What's my gift?" I guess it's just in the last few years that I've realized this is it. It gives me goose bumps. I have a passion for teaching, and I never want to stop doing it.

> —STACEY McMULLEN,
> *Texas Region XI Secondary Teacher of the Year*

Teaching is a profession of compassion, creativity, discipline, problem-solving, personal growth, and wonder. There is no greater task than educating our children for participation in a free, democratic society.

> —BETSY GLISSON,
> *Harris County, Ohio, Teacher of the Year*

I understood, after I had my first class of third-graders. . . . that I truly had fulfilled what I wanted to be. I was a movie star—I had my own stage there and a captive audience. I have a mission to stretch those children's minds, so I am a missionary. And I diagnose problems and give solutions. I've fulfilled a childhood dream.

> —AMY BYRD,
>   *Rockwall, Texas, Elementary Teacher of the Year*

The complexity of teaching is a challenge worthy of the greatest efforts and dedication. No two days are the same. Each day I laugh at something; some days I cry.

> —*Vermont's* MICHELE FORMAN,
>   *National Teacher of the Year*

If teachers really take their job seriously, they can really make a difference in a kid's life. You really touch a life—you are molding someone. That's better than any other job I know of, and I take my responsibility seriously. I know it sounds corny, but I just can't wait to get to school in the morning.

> —LEE DANIEL KENT, *Virginia Teacher of the Year*

I think I'll always be a teacher, whether I want to be or not. It seems to be an involuntary reflex I have.

> —LOUISE DURHAM, *Utah Teacher of the Year*

This is really one of the only jobs that you can truly see how you're improving year by year. You can see it in how children change through the course of the year, and how they grow and how some of the ones who are having a difficult time can get better. My students tend to be a reflection of me, of how I am, so I try to be the right example for them. One day, I hope to be really, really good at this.

> —PAUL RATCLIFF, *Chesapeake, Virginia,*
> *Elementary Teacher of the Year*

There aren't too many jobs where you can take your life experiences and work them into your job performance, and I can.

> —MAUREEN HOFFMANN, *Iowa Teacher of the Year*

I was taught that it is not enough just to live my life. I was placed on this planet to make a difference in the lives of others.

> —EDWARD J. SILVER JR.,
> *Maryland Teacher of the Year*

Teaching is a timeless profession. It is the basis of all other professions. Good teachers plant the seeds that

make good doctors, good accountants, good public
servants, good statesmen, good taxi drivers, and
good astronauts. When former students return to see
me over the years, my heart fills up in the
knowledge that I have been part of the wonderful
accumulation of experiences that followed them
though life.

> —*Virginia's* MARY V. BICOUVARIS,
> *National Teacher of the Year*

Being a good teacher comes from the heart.

> —BARBARA DORFF,
> *Texas Secondary Teacher of the Year*

There is almost a selfish feeling of wellness and self
worth that is achieved personally while working
with children. It allows for personal growth while
serving society, a rare combination of Mother Teresa
and Lewis and Clark.

> —JOANNE GUAY, *Ohio Teacher of the Year*

I had to do a lot of soul-searching to decide what I
wanted to do with my life. When my first child was
born I instantly knew. He was like a sponge and I

was amazed at the learning process, and I just knew that this was what I was supposed to do with my life.

—KAREN NORTON, *Arkansas Teacher of the Year*

My classroom is as varied as the days of the year and the lives of the children that inhabit it.

—JAN COLEMAN-KNIGHT,
    Alameda County, California, Teacher of the Year

Every day, it's different. When you go in with a lesson and you don't know how it's going to end up and you don't know how the kids are going to react to it—every day is just fun that way.

—JOAN KNISS, *Colorado Teacher of the Year*

I pray every morning that I can touch at least one life.

—DEBORAH PARROTT,
    Texas Region VI Secondary Teacher of the Year

Many teachers make a difference, and you realize how much by the students who come back and tell us. For instance, a girl now in 11th grade came back and told me, "You taught me the love of poetry." That means a lot.

—CAROLE FIRESTONE, *California Teacher of the Year*

The wonderful thing about teaching is that the more you put into it, the more you get back.

—RICHARD SPRECHER, *Montgomery County, Maryland, Teacher of the Year*

As Americans, the most formidable weapon we have in our arsenal is education. There is nothing more patriotic that one can do in his career or her career than become a teacher.

—*California's* CHAUNCEY VEATCH, *National Teacher of the Year*

It's All About the Kids

A deep, genuine love of children is what guides me.

> —MARJORIE CORRELL, *Educator of the Year in*
> *Colorado's Harrison School District Two*

You really have to use your heart to understand
students, to know what's going on inside them and
how to reach them.

> —VICKI DONOVAN,
> *New Hampshire Teacher of the Year*

To be an outstanding teacher. . . . a person must
possess an unconditional love for teaching children.
Teaching children is a passion that needs to run
through your veins every time you step in front of
the class.

> —THOMAS ESPARZA III,
> *New Mexico Teacher of the Year*

Sometimes I want to kill my students, and some days
they want to kill me. But I am proud of what they
have done and where they have gone.

> —LEE T. "PETE" PEDERSEN,
> *Maine Teacher of the Year*

If you don't love kids you don't belong in teaching.
That's the bottom line. We're a people business.

> —PAUL BLACK,
> *Pennsylvania Teacher Educator of the Year*

My favorite part of the day is the minute the
kindergarteners walk in the room. A quiet, cold
space becomes immediately filled with the
excitement of a new day, full of voices, boo-boos,
laughter, and learning.

> —REBECCA O'CONNELL, *Teacher of the Year at
> Citrus County, Florida's Inverness Primary School*

The first couple of days of class I don't teach, I
interview the students. I say "Tell me about yourself,
favorite teacher from last year, what did you have for
breakfast today?" It's kind of a slow start to school,
but we make it up. When I say, "How are you
doing?" they know I mean it. Kids will learn from
someone they want to learn from.

> —ROGER HUBERTY, *Wisconsin Teacher of the Year*

They're so young and so excited and everything is
new to them. And it's just so neat, just to watch

them grow. And they love you. Especially the little ones, they all love you. You can have bad hair and they still love you.

—JAN GERICK,
    Plano, Texas, Elementary Teacher of the Year

Kids don't leave or enter my classroom without getting a hug from me. It's dangerous for teachers to touch their students, but I've always done it. We need to take the time to touch these kids' lives—literally—and take the time to reach the kids who seem unreachable.

—JUDY BIEZE, *Idaho Teacher of the Year*

After all is said and done, an outstanding teacher is still willing to hold her students in her arms when they need a hug and say, "I want you to succeed because I care," knowing full well it may be years before any of those students return to say thanks. But when they do, it is the greatest reward of all.

—CANDACE BUTLER,
    South Bend, Indiana, Teacher of the Year

Each and every day we as teachers have a chance to be part of the miracle of growth and development of the young people who will be the future of our community.

> —HARRIET PAUL JONQUIERE,
> *New York Teacher of the Year*

Teaching is the most noble profession. I can leave here, even on the worst day, knowing I have done my best to engage kids. Every day is different, every day a kid makes a comment you haven't heard before, or a kid who hasn't made any comment suddenly connects to something. And I'm thinking, "Wow, I had some part in that."

> —DAVID LUSSIER, *Massachusetts Teacher of the Year*

The best part of my job is to get to spend my day with kids. They keep me thinking young.

> —SUSAN M. RIPPE, *Kansas Teacher of the Year*

When you get to know children's families, you don't want to leave because you want to teach their brothers and sisters.

> —KAREN SEXTON,
> *Teacher of the Year at Greensboro, North Carolina's Johnson Street Elementary*

I remain enthusiastic because I don't think there's any other job that is so different from day to day. This job is an adventure, bringing together students from all walks of life, from various cultures and traditions from around the world. And sometimes, these students leave you with a smile at the end of the day, and that certainly makes you want to continue. I have some of my former students' children as my students now, and I tell you, it's a thrilling feeling, knowing that I have taught their parents in the past.

—PATRICIA GOODNIGHT,
  Washington, D.C., Teacher of the Year

One of the things I really love about teaching is that no two days are ever alike. Every day there are new issues and new ideas and new perspectives. It's a very exciting thing to catch that magic moment when a kid says, "Yeah, I got it." It's a gratifying job.

—MAUREEN WHELAN SPAIGHT,
  Rhode Island Teacher of the Year

More than anything else, I enjoy seeing the spark come on for the first time. You can tell the second they see their own personal growth, you can see it come over their faces. It beams like a ray of light.

—DEBORAH JOHNSTON, *Colorado Teacher of the Year*

The biggest kick in teaching comes when I look into the face of a young child and watch confusion turn to concentration, concentration to surprise, and finally, surprise into the pride of accomplishment.

—*Georgia's* ANDY BAUMGARTNER, *National Teacher of the Year*

The accomplishments that I value most are those that cannot be captured by a line on a résumé or recognized by a plaque. The intense joy and satisfaction that I get from seeing one of my new soccer players score her first goal or helping a professed non-reader connect with a really great story or assisting a young writer in playing with the language on the page until his poem is just right— these are the accomplishments that motivate me on a daily basis to continue pursuing my goal to earn that title of utmost distinction: teacher.

—MARTHA STICKLE, *Teacher of the Year for Louisiana's Ascension Parish*

What excites me about teaching is the work my
students do, the discoveries they make each day. . . .
I see myself as a coach and a resource for my
students. I am a provider of opportunities, but the
work is theirs and it is truly remarkable.

> —NANCY BRENNAN,
> *New Hampshire Teacher of the Year*

The rewards I find in teaching are many and varied.
The moment a child grasps a concept that has been a
mystery is surely one of the most rewarding.

> —SUSAN BARRETT,
> *West Virginia Teacher of the Year*

It is the students who make us who we are.

> —TALITA DENEGRI, *Oklahoma Teacher of the Year*

My students have taught me everything I know
about teaching. I learn a strategy and they, without
knowing it, allow me to see if I am a believer in that
technique. I then analyze the information to make
learning better for my students. I am the teacher I
am because my students have molded me.

> —TONYA PERRY, *Alabama Teacher of the Year*

What makes someone a great teacher is honestly their students. If your students don't laugh at your corny jokes, aren't enthusiastic about your teaching style, and aren't receptive, it's tough.

> —SALLY PONCE-O'ROURKE, *Teacher of the Year at California's Moorpark College*

It's the work of the students that makes me shine. It's their success that I pride myself on.

> —TODD FIELDS, *Maine Teacher of the Year*

In giving all we have to them, we also learn so much from them. And that is why I teach. Had I chosen another profession, I would have missed all the wonderful young people it has been my privilege to know.

> —MARIANNE MORAN, *Massachusetts Teacher of the Year*

One of the most important things a teacher can offer a student is a relationship with an adult. I don't presume to know more of anything than they do, except to be older. We talk and sometimes we disagree. But it's a relationship. They must feel that they're welcome.

> —*Minnesota's* MARY BETH BLEGEN,
>   *National Teacher of the Year*

The relationships I have developed with my students are among the accomplishments I value most. I take great pride in seeing my former students succeed in their chosen fields and encourage them to come back to share their experiences with current students who are considering what to do with their lives.

> —EDE ASHWORTH,
>   *West Virginia Teacher of the Year*

The relationship between teacher and student does not end when they leave you. It is a long-lasting relationship.

> —CELINE ROBERTSON, *Nebraska Teacher of the Year*

We must reinforce the human aspects of education, so we do not become computer-like in an age of computers.

> —*Connecticut's* LEROY E. HAY,
>   *National Teacher of the Year*

Kids need a classroom to learn where they're loved unconditionally but at the same time they're given very firm boundaries, where they can make mistakes in a non-threatening atmosphere. If kids feel that their teacher loves them and supports them, then that's where they're going to blossom.

—KELLY BARREIRA,
  San Clemente, California, Teacher of the Year

I wouldn't be able to teach children anything without a positive rapport. They have to know you really care about them.

—AMY MONROE DENTY,
  Georgia Teacher of the Year

Doing what I can to help others be their best, I think, is my greatest contribution to education. With my students, I try very hard to give them the motivation and self-confidence to stretch and grow and become the best they can. I love when I go to the regional volleyball game at 7 a.m., and they wave at me before a serve. I like when I see them at Safeway, and they introduce me to their friends rather than ducking down the canned food aisle.

—JOAN KNISS, *Colorado Teacher of the Year*

Every time I walk into any school or see children at the store or the fair, I have a profound sense of honor that I have the job I do that brings me such pleasure, and that I am good at, too.

—CINDY GULISANO, *Wyoming Teacher of the Year*

Degrees and certificates aside, being in the classroom and working with young hearts and minds is my accomplishment.

—EILEEN THORNBURGH, *Idaho Teacher of the Year*

I look up to people like Martin Luther King and Robert Kennedy, people who do for other people. Women in nuclear freeze groups, 70-year-old women who lay down on railroad tracks. I want to be that kind of role model. My students come first and the subject matter second. There is a lot of respect, caring, and empathy. Everything I do is predicated on this.

—CAROL VIROSTEK, *Connecticut Teacher of the Year*

Having kids has helped me a lot, because I see the kids I have in class and remind myself, "These are someone's kids, just like mine." And I know in a few

years I'll be the one on the other side, asking a
teacher questions about how they're doing.

—Sharon Cournoyer,
Windsor Locks, Connecticut, Teacher of the Year

Even though I am a service-oriented person, I never
dreamed that the hugs and smiles of the children I
work with could boost my self-esteem and make me
feel so good about the work I enjoy.

—Judith Moore,
Polk County, Florida, Teacher of the Year

I want students to know that I care what they do
with their lives. My fellow teachers and I put success
on their minds, and then push, shake, cajole, shout,
and sometimes even force success into them.

—Emiel Hamberlin, *Illinois Teacher of the Year*

I care about you as a person and I will do everything
in my power to help you be a success now or ten
years from now. You are my students for life
whether you like it or not.

—Michael B. Kaiser, *Indiana Teacher of the Year,
on what he tells students*

The end result of any education reform must be the child. Each child must be given the very best education that we are capable of giving.

> —MARIANNE MORAN,
> *Massachusetts Teacher of the Year*

My first responsibility is to kids—to who they are and to who they can become. I can only hope that in the time we spend together, I can help them find joy in discovery and learning, but most importantly, joy in themselves.

> —*Minnesota's* MARY BETH BLEGEN,
> *National Teacher of the Year*

I could never be without children. The day I'm forced to retire, when I'm really old, I'll come back as a volunteer. . . . I could never picture myself not being in front of a classroom.

> —MARILYN MISA, *Teacher of the Year for the
> Catholic Diocese of Raleigh, North Carolina*

The flow of warmth and affection between teacher and student as well as between student and student creates an atmosphere of mutual acceptance in which teaching and learning flourish. . . . To create such an environment is one of the most important goals a teacher can pursue.

—*New York's* JAY SOMMER,
National Teacher of the Year

I don't think there is anything greater than seeing a child leave my room and school, at the end of the day, proudly carrying their artwork home to anxiously show their siblings and parents.

—DENISE RIGAUD, *Teacher of the Year at Hernando County, Florida's J. D. Floyd Elementary*

Imagine if we loved other people's children enough to do what we would do for our own—to fight for them, to protect them, to work to give them the best of everything. That level of compassion takes courage—political courage, financial courage, and emotional courage. It takes courage to act on what we know is best for children—to dig in our heels and say no to bad decisions, to risk condemnation or even our jobs to support what we know is right for children. The real heroes in education are the people willing to take a stand for what is right.

—MARIAN GALBRAITH,
Connecticut Teacher of the Year

Metaphorically Speaking

Education is the most important tool for our children.

> —CAROLYN PINCKNEY,
>   *Washington, D.C., Teacher of the Year*

Teaching is brain surgery without breaking the skin. It should not be entered into lightly nor performed by amateurs.

> —DANIEL WALKER, *Alaska Teacher of the Year*

Everything we do in our lives as teachers is like a spinning spiral because we touch students, parents, colleagues, and strangers, and we become more astute, more caring, and better educators.

> —*California's* MARILYN JACHETTI WHIRRY,
>   *National Teacher of the Year*

Life is a huge relay race. I am alive and carrying the baton now. The future depends on me as surely as my generation depended on our teachers and their teachers and their teachers.

> —ELLEN KEMPLER, *Florida Teacher of the Year*

I cannot be a vending machine that dispenses information. All we can do is give students the tools to go out and learn for themselves.

—NANCY McROBERTS, *Kansas Teacher of the Year*

What a gift it is to be a teacher. I will never be a movie star—but quite frankly, Kevin Costner will never teach fifth grade, either.

—LEONARD SWANTON,
Massachusetts Teacher of the Year

Society needs education's product—well-honed minds—but it does little to encourage our system of production.

—*West Virginia's* RAE ELLEN McKEE,
National Teacher of the Year

The most important things teachers impart are not only written on assessment quizzes, but written on the hearts of children.

—JUDY JOERDING, *Teacher of the Year for Missouri's Ferguson-Florissant School District*

Like Jimmy Stewart's character George Bailey in *It's a Wonderful Life*, teachers are often faced with the questions, "Do I matter? Has my time in the classroom been worth it? Have I made a difference in the life of a young person?" As a teacher, I rarely see immediate job satisfaction. Often it takes years, if at all, when I hear from a former student reminding me that, yes, I have made a difference.

> —RICK AHERNS, *Teacher of the Year at Hernando County, Florida's Hernando High*

We're not just teachers, we're educational artists. We paint young minds.

> —VINA BARR, *Lake County, Florida, Teacher of the Year*

In being a good teacher you have to be a little bit of Dr. Faustus and Peter Pan. I have an unquenchable thirst to know more, but I also want to have fun.

> —MAUREEN WHELAN SPAIGHT, *Rhode Island Teacher of the Year*

The process of teaching is, in itself, an art form. Meaningful teaching, like meaningful art, requires inspiration and imagination, communication and interpretation, and the ongoing pursuit of growth and understanding.

—SHEILA F. WARNER, *Chapel Hill–Carrboro, North Carolina, Teacher of the Year*

Children are the hidden treasures that we're reaching for behind the thorns; and they've hidden themselves very well behind timidity, fear, low self-esteem, failure, and sadness. It is our responsibility to find the right way to teach them.

—MARY MORELAND, *Muscogee County, Ohio, Teacher of the Year*

Most teachers are neither illiterates nor miracle workers, but dedicated laborers in the vineyards of students' hearts and minds.

—BRUCE M. PENNIMAN, *Massachusetts Teacher of the Year*

There are three kinds of kids: swan divers, swimmers who cling to kickboards, and those who refuse to get in the water. I always teach to the swan divers. I don't teach to the ones who will sit on the side of the pool, but I empower those kids to know where the kickboards are.

—JANIS HEIGL,
    Southwest Washington Teacher of the Year

Within each person there is an essential core that I try to touch. It's like the farmer plowing the field. With each turn of the disk he changes the dirt, and while I may not get to see the harvest, I still turn the disk.

—CATHY BISSOONDIAL, *Illinois Teacher of the Year*

Just as individual instruments combine to form a symphony, our goal is to develop the potential of each student in order to contribute to the overall good of the community.

—PAULINE WILLIAMS, *San Diego County, California, Teacher of the Year*

I feel less like a teacher and more like a traveling companion on what I hope will be a pleasant and exciting journey.

—DEBI BARRETT-HAYES, *Florida Teacher of the Year*

We must decide if we want education to create cogs in the wheel of success, or if we want education to help human beings become human. Education provides things that you can't sell on a world market, like music, the ability to relate to people, the ability to enjoy life.

—*West Virginia's* RAE ELLEN MCKEE,
National Teacher of the Year

It is a joy for me to go into the classroom. I want to challenge other educators: Look at your children not as vessels to be filled, but as candles to be lit.

—KAREN NORTON, *Arkansas Teacher of the Year*

All children are gifted, and it's up to us teachers to open the door to that giftedness. It's up to every one of us educators to open every door to every child. It's simply not enough to be the giver of knowledge. We must not only fill the pails with knowledge, but light the fire of enthusiasm.

—SHARON IVIE, *Colorado Teacher of the Year*

My classroom is not pretty. As classrooms go, it's probably the worst room in the school. But it is a metaphor for the lessons I teach my kids. Look past the surface, past the cracked walls, the clogged sinks, and the dust. If you look beyond, you can see so much more.

—*New Jersey's* TERRI GRAHAM,
    Disney American Teacher Award Honoree

Life's a journey, not a guided tour. My role as a teacher is to help students take pride in their journey, ask questions, search for answers and learn from mistakes. I want my students to actively set goals and pursue them. I don't want them to be content as passive observers as life passes them by.

—SHARON COURNOYER,
    Windsor Locks, Connecticut, Teacher of the Year

Long Hours, Low Pay, Priceless Rewards

Teaching is a lot of hard work and a lot of challenges, but I don't think people realize just how much fun teaching is. Every day of teaching is a good day for me.

> —TAMMY DUEHR,
> *Dubuque, Iowa, Teacher of the Year*

People call me a workaholic, but I get a lot out of it. I get the same thrill now in the classroom as I did as a little girl playing school.

> —GAIL JOHNSON,
> *Cherokee County, Florida, Teacher of the Year*

Even when I'm not teaching, I'm thinking about it. I'll be playing a game with friends and think, "How can I work this into teaching?" The job is never done with me.

> —BARBARA EVERSON,
> *Coeur d'Alene, Idaho, Educator of the Year*

The part that I was not aware of when I went into the profession is how difficult it is, how much time it takes, and how wrong the public perception is. You say, "Oh, teachers have their summers off," and I tell you I haven't had a summer off since 1978 and neither have most of my colleagues. Most teachers use the summer to write curricula, update their skills, take a course. Teaching isn't a profession. It's a vocation.

—MARIANNE MORAN,
Massachusetts Teacher of the Year

Teaching is portrayed a lot of times as a hard job, but for me it's just a pleasure. It really doesn't feel like a job. Working with kids is so much fun. Who wouldn't want to do it?

—TRACY CALLARD, *Kansas Teacher of the Year*

They say our job is teaching. We know that our life is teaching. Every time we walk into our classrooms we have to be ready to do so much more than teach.

—*Minnesota's* MARY BETH BLEGEN,
National Teacher of the Year

Teachers wear a lot of hats. It's an extremely draining job. It's like being a parent to 25 kids. I don't know what profession has a greater impact on society than teaching, and yet teachers are held in such low esteem. They are under-appreciated, underpaid, and disrespected. If you want the best people, then there are going to have to be changes, salary changes, changes in attitude. At my school there are cars in the parking lot at 7 A.M., then at 5:30 at night there are still teachers there working with students. People think teachers work 9 to 3. And I have to tell you, I didn't know it myself. I used to say "What a racket!"

—BARBARA LASARACINA,
New Jersey Teacher of the Year

When I get overwhelmed by paperwork, I go read with a child and I remember why I went into this profession.

—MINDY REED, *Union County, North Carolina, Teacher of the Year*

It's a very hard profession. It's very tiring, and it can be very frustrating because your expectations are very high. But it's fun.

—DEBORAH WHITE, *Oregon Teacher of the Year*

The road is often long, difficult. and filled with frustrations. However, the challenges and rewards cannot be equaled. The joy we feel at seeing a student's face light up with excitement about what he is learning is unparalleled.

—*South Carolina's* TERRY KNECHT DOZIER,
National Teacher of the Year

My idea of a Teacher of the Year is not one with papers piled high that need to be graded. I think I'm like all teachers. I work as hard as I can, and I wish I could do more with 24 hours than I'm able to do.

—LOUISE DURHAM, *Utah Teacher of the Year*

I worry about prospective teachers who think, "Why am I going into this? It's going to be long hours for low pay and I'm going to get bashed." But being inside, I think this is the most exciting time to be in education.

—DAVID LUSSIER, *Massachusetts Teacher of the Year*

Teachers are being worked to death with the constant stress of too many papers and too much grading. The greatest asset a teacher has is time and there is never enough of it. There is a great scene in the film *Mr. Holland's Opus* when Mr. Holland tells an experienced teacher that he is going to write his great symphony during his spare time while teaching. Every teacher who sees this movie laughs knowingly at the statement.

> —*Virginia's* PHILIP BIGLER,
>   *National Teacher of the Year*

People ask me, "How can you keep doing this?" But I don't teach curriculum. The curriculum would get old. I teach kids, and you get 52 new ones a year.

> —JANIS HEIGL,
>   *Southwest Washington Teacher of the Year*

Teaching is something you live. You live teaching, and that means that almost every experience you have, everything you read, or every artifact you come across, you find yourself thinking about how you can utilize this in your classroom. It becomes a part of your life. If I am a creative teacher, and I think I am, it's because I read incessantly and I'm excited about ideas, even after 30 years.

> —FRANK D. GAWLE, *Connecticut Teacher of the Year*

Remember why you became a teacher. When you are working long hours while your friends enjoy 40-

hour weeks, and you don't think you can endure much longer, remember why you are in that classroom. You are in that classroom because you love your subject and you love kids. You are a cultivator of minds, a shaper of nations. You are not just a teacher.

—LEE SILVA,
Plano, Texas, Secondary Teacher of the Year

I found it to be the hardest job I've ever done. It is a 24-hour job, seven days a week, all year round.

—MARIANNE MORAN,
Massachusetts Teacher of the Year

Good teachers are basically born good teachers. You can't learn it. You have to really like the material, the content. A lot of people get burned out after a few years because of the paperwork. I think you need to keep in mind why you chose this profession—to make a difference in someone's life—not for monetary reasons. Higher salaries would help, though. I think more people would consider teaching if salaries were more competitive.

—BILL RICHEY, *Ohio Teacher of the Year*

There are areas where teachers are under stress, and some of them we can't control. Control of your salary is one of them. To support my family, I work an additional 15 hours a week as a mechanic. We don't have the prestige position teachers used to hold. The schools have somehow lost respect. The only way we are going to get it back is to work for it.

—ROBERT TRAYNOR, *Arizona Teacher of the Year*

Teachers who really care are not in this for the income; we're in this for the outcome.

—RICH RUFFALO, *New Jersey Teacher of the Year*

There are three types of teachers: winners, whiners, and wieners. When you teach and you have that passion, you really don't get tired. The wieners don't teach with passion. They don't volunteer for anything. They don't get involved. They don't go that extra mile.

—PATRICIA AVALLONE,
    Connecticut Teacher of the Year

Educators make a difference in this nation, in the lives of children every day. There's got to be a way that we can bring up not only the teacher pay raises, but the morale of educators. Because our salaries are so low, that tends to bring morale down, and that's detrimental to the kids.

—KAREN NORTON, *Arkansas Teacher of the Year*

In a society that often measures success by the size of a paycheck, we sometimes feel disenfranchised and unappreciated, but we must not lose our focus. In a society that too often measures student success by standardized test scores, we sometimes feel constrained, but we must not lose our vision.

—ANITA MEYER MEINBACH,
Miami-Dade County, Florida, Teacher of the Year

There are internal rewards to teaching that can't be accomplished with a paycheck. Somehow you live on through your students. What better things can be said about a human being but that he touched a lot of lives?

—*Tennessee's* TERRY WEEKS,
National Teacher of the Year

No monetary figure can be assigned to reward a teacher for reaching a reluctant learner, counseling a child at risk, or giving a student the gift of a lifelong love and enthusiasm for learning.

—CARLA CALDERON,
    Katy, Texas, Elementary Teacher of the Year

Money and fame are not part of this profession. But the things teachers do will affect, long-term, the course of civilization. Teachers are planting seeds. . . . It's a dance, a tradition that goes back centuries. We are all students and you never know who is going to pass the torch to you.

—MARK DAMEN, *Utah Teacher of the Year*

Your reward for being a good teacher is to move into administration. . . . I was offered a job as a supervisor, at double the salary. Call me dumb, but I stayed in the classroom because that's the most important place to be. It's the greatest job in the world. I wouldn't want to lose it.

—JEFF JOHNSTON, *Nevada Teacher of the Year*

I know it sounds kind of trite, but if I didn't need a paycheck to survive, I would do this for free. There are so many teachers who feel that way about their profession.

—MARIA FRONTAIN, *Arizona Teacher of the Year*

If you're looking for compensation you shouldn't be teaching. Some people play golf. I teach.

—SHERYL NUSSBAUM-BEACH, *Virginia Beach, Virginia, Teacher of the Year*

If you are doing it for the money, you are in the wrong business. It's the challenge of working with students and the student who says, "I thought it would be difficult, but you make it interesting." Once or twice year, a student will say, "I like science and will take more"—or kids who say, "I'm majoring in chemistry because of you." You can't eat it, or buy anything with that, but that's the best part.

—DARWIN OCHS, *Antelope Valley, California, Teacher of the Year*

The rewards that keep us in this business are the notes from children who say you're the best teacher in the world, the little hugs you get each day, and notes from parents that say how much they appreciate you. That's what keeps you going. The rewards are incredible.

—JUDITH SOLOVEY,
    Hamilton County, Tennessee, Teacher of the Year

I get very tired, but I'm back at it Monday morning. I love teaching. I've never been bored.

—*Minnesota's* MARY BETH BLEGEN,
    National Teacher of the Year

A good teacher smiles while she's teaching. She smiles because she is comfortable not only with her subject matter, but also with her classroom and her students. She smiles because children respond quicker to encouragement rather than disparagement. And she smiles because at the end of a very long day, with papers to grade, and forms to fill out, and meetings to attend, a child may peek his head in the door and say, "We gonna write poems like that again tomorrow? That was fun!" That is when I smile.

—*Ohio's* SHARON M. DRAPER,
    National Teacher of the Year

I want you to go back to your schools and find another one of us who is thinking about resigning, because we have a hard profession, and I want you to show them what you already know: That teaching is a great profession.

—CONNIE HINES,
  Broward County, Florida, Teacher of the Year

Professional Development Tips from the Pros

To improve education, teachers need to keep improving themselves.

—ERIN HILL, *Nevada Teacher of the Year*

About five years ago, I was the model teacher: stand, lecture, put the formula on the chalkboard, do the recipe, experiment, test, grade. I realized that if I'm average, my kids are average. I had to raise the bar.

—RICK ESPINOZA,
New Mexico Science Teacher of the Year

I'm always learning; you're never done being a student. Society is always changing. As a teacher . . . if you're not willing to learn yourself, you'll be left behind.

—NANCY MCROBERTS, *Kansas Teacher of the Year*

I always try to do something different each year because it's important for me to stay fresh. Most good teachers feel a bit of guilt if they find themselves teaching something the same way they did last year.

—STEVEN LEVY, *Massachusetts Teacher of the Year*

I continue to learn. I hope all teachers continue to learn. To just collect a paycheck is terrible.

—TERRI K. FISHBOUGH,
Tulare County, California, Teacher of the Year

Most teachers possess academic competence in their subject areas, but not all possess academic enthusiasm.

—*Florida's* TRACEY L. BAILEY,
National Teacher of the Year

I still consider myself a rookie, after 30 years in the business. When I drive down that hill to school every day, I still have a nervous edge. I think you need to operate in this business with some kind of little nervous edge—to know you're prepared, that teaching is still important, that it's still exciting.

—FRANK D. GAWLE, *Connecticut Teacher of the Year*

A good teacher has to adapt to change. You have to keep abreast of what's going on and bring it to the classroom. Young teachers need to get out in the field, to be involved in what's happening in their communities. Student teachers are our best resource.

I was told that a long time ago, and I'll never forget it. Engage in conversations with diverse groups of people. Many of the positive and constructive things we can do as educators don't have to cost money.

—DOROTHY NEAL, *Maine Teacher of the Year*

Teachers have to provide balance and consistency in a world where students' home life changes rapidly. They have to know that "new" is not necessarily better, but can be. They must develop knowledge, not as a necessity to do their work, but as a way of life.

—LEONARD SWANTON,
Massachusetts Teacher of the Year

When teachers find out what other teachers are doing, that's truly exciting. We can learn from each other.

—MARGARET HOLTSCHLAG,
Michigan Teacher of the Year

I am always eager to hear about any idea that other educators have tried and found to be successful. I never stop at the expected, but try to push myself and my students to want to know and do more.

—LAURIE SYBERT, *Missouri Teacher of the Year*

I have to be a learner to keep up with new methods that are out there and new ways of helping children learn. Another goal is to be a mentor. I enjoy being a mentor to college students or other teachers within the school. The ultimate goal is to help the children with their writing, reading, arithmetic, science, or socially.

—SUZANNE LULL,
        New Hampshire Teacher of the Year

A teacher who understands the dynamic nature of the profession will continue to develop and grow professionally. Often a teacher forgets that many things have changed since he received his degree: new and additional learning strategies, a changed student population. Last year's lesson plans or examinations carefully filed away for future use may no longer be relevant in next year's class.

—*New York's* JAY SOMMER,
        National Teacher of the Year

I really don't know that I do things out of the ordinary. I observe that which works for other teachers. I try to incorporate that into my own teaching, and I share it.

> —*Texas's* JOHNNIE ENG,
> *American Association of Teachers of Spanish and Portuguese Spanish Teacher of the Year*

If a teacher just stays within the four walls of their classroom, they'll go insane.

> —MIKE BYNUM, *Oklahoma Teacher of the Year*

How can we hope to hold our students to higher standards if we don't hold teachers to higher standards?

> —*Vermont's* MICHELE FORMAN,
> *National Teacher of the Year*

The more knowledge we have, the better educators we become.

> —BETH REYNOLDS, *Missouri Teacher of the Year*

If we choose to deny the need for accountability, we are merely opening the doors wider for criticism and disruption. If we make excuses and become defensive in the face of suggested accountability measures, we are asking for more scrutiny from those who don't really understand. . . . We must work toward a system where we are accountable to each other in our own buildings, districts, and states.

> —*Minnesota's* MARY BETH BLEGEN,
> *National Teacher of the Year*

As teachers, we are going to have to reevaluate everything we teach and see what students will need as adults. We can't assume what we consider valuable today will have a relevance to students 50 years from now. We have to stop, clean off the plate, and start from scratch. It's scary, but exciting.

> —MARY THOREEN, *Teacher of the Year at Tampa,*
> *Florida's Wilson Middle School*

Often, teachers just quietly teach and let others try and implement change. But we have to take a leadership role; when we see good ideas that we need implemented, we've got to do it instead of sitting around and waiting.

> —CAROL BANASZYNSKI,
> *Wisconsin Teacher of the Year*

Find a mentor and don't be afraid to use that mentor. Whether you come into teaching at 21, at 30, or in your 40s or 50s, the hardest thing is to be a novice. In this business, the years of experience make a difference.

—MARIANNE MORAN,
Massachusetts Teacher of the Year

Teaching can be very lonely. When the classroom door is closed, teachers are in their own world. Forming communities of teachers can break this isolation.

—*Vermont's* MICHELE FORMAN,
National Teacher of the Year

When I entered the profession, a fellow teacher told me that most teachers stop changing after three years. I am not sure of the statement's validity; however, I take it as a serious threat. I see teaching as forever evolving, just as our understanding of learning will invariably change and improve. If I fail to keep up, I fail as a teacher, I fail my students, and I fail the cause of education. Instead, I choose to grow.

—DEREK K. MINAKAMI, *Hawaii Teacher of the Year*

While trends and legislation make their marks on the educational process, what one does in the classroom is evolutionary. The teacher I am today is a compilation of continued training, personal and professional reading, and learning from many outstanding teachers.

—MARGIE YURTINUS, *Teacher of the Year at Hernando County, Florida's Suncoast Elementary*

Creating
Lifelong Learners

If I can encourage a lifelong curiosity in my students, I believe they will have a much better chance at success, happiness, and strong relationships with others in their own lives.

> —VIRGINIA MAXFIELD,
> *Decatur, Georgia, Teacher of the Year*

Create a comfortable and safe environment where kids are willing to risk. Then, education has a whole new meaning for them because it's something they're actively involved in.

> —LYNNE M. ELLIS,
> *New Hampshire Teacher of the Year*

My goal for the students is to prepare them to be successful 30-year-olds. If I can manage to do a good job of what I'm here to do, then the results will be felt in the lives of these children, and in the people they touch.

> —LINDA ADAMSON, *Maryland Teacher of the Year*

What you have to do is instill enthusiasm in kids. If I can get their attention and they like what they're doing, then they will go on to do more. You have to hear from them. They want to hear their own voices; they need to gain confidence. I want them to know that what matters is their ideas and how they present them.

> —*Minnesota's* MARY BETH BLEGEN,
> *National Teacher of the Year*

All children deserve to be taught in an environment that will promote, value, and nurture their natural desire to learn.

> —SUSIE HAAS, *California Teacher of the Year*

Young children don't have a large frame of reference, so they learn best by touching, and by feeling themselves to be a part of what they're studying. I don't believe in just memorizing facts— and I think that's important for adults, too.

> —CAROL OPPENHEIM,
> *Humane Society of Missouri Teacher of the Year*

To open the minds and spirits of our young people, we must help them feel love for the search for knowledge—a search to know the what and the why, to understand the hearts and minds of others, and to understand the meaning of the world and our place in it.

> —*California's* MARILYN JACHETTI WHIRRY,
> *National Teacher of the Year*

It's not enough to be a cheerleader. You've got to hook students, engage and involve them in the learning process. My classroom operates as a professor working with graduate students. It's an energetic, productive atmosphere. It's charged . . . with the energy of real, productive learning, real, productive experiments.

> —*Florida's* TRACEY L. BAILEY,
> *National Teacher of the Year*

I'm big on working through play. We need to let children discover. You don't want to take that away from them.

> —STEVEN HICKS,
> *Los Angeles County Teacher of the Year*

The kids like my teaching style. It's pretty loose, pretty interactive. I encourage my students to "think out of the box" and, as a result, I produce students who leave my class as critical thinkers, analytical writers, and involved citizens. Establishing a positive learning environment is more than just establishing rules and procedures. Students must feel free to express opinions and believe that their opinions are valued.

> —DIANNA MILLER,
> *Clay County, Florida, Teacher of the Year*

If children can grow to love learning, enjoy the quest for knowledge, and treasure the discoveries they make along the way, then I have been a success.

> —DIANE BAILEY, *Teacher of the Year for*
> *California's Fountain Valley School District*

I admit if I don't know something or have to think about the question. I sit back and say, "Mmmm, I'm not sure." I'm not the answer man.

> —GERHARD ALMS,
> *Orange County, California,*
> *Teacher of the Year*

A teacher must present himself to the students as a professional who accepts hard work and then is able

to demonstrate the rewards attainable when hard
work is met head on.

> —JOHN KEON,
>   *Pasco County, Florida, Teacher of the Year*

Exploring knowledge requires a non-threatening
classroom atmosphere, which I believe is central to a
healthy classroom climate. I want students to feel
free to make mistakes, and then learn from those
mistakes. In this kind of climate, a learner can
venture to be creative, involved, and self-motivated.

> —JANICE HUDSON,
>   *Muscogee County, Georgia, Teacher of the Year*

Inquiry and discovery are very important to me. I
try to let students make a lot of the choices and
decisions. I try to let them discover things on their
own and then help them build on those discoveries.

> —AMY MONROE DENTY,
>   *Georgia Teacher of the Year*

Teachers play an extremely important role in the
lives of students. For some, teachers may be the only
stable adults in their lives. Teachers may be their
only hope for a better future. When teachers are

asked what they want for their students as they become adults, the responses usually include wanting the students to be responsible, productive citizens who are lifelong learners. If this is the philosophy by which we teach, then shouldn't it be the philosophy by which we live?

—CARYN ELLISON,
   Mishawaka, Indiana, Teacher of the Year

People learn more when they're having fun. My goal in teaching has always been not to teach like I was taught, but like I wish I had been taught.

—TOM TURPIN, *Indiana Professor of the Year*

Students should have the opportunity to see, hear, feel, taste, and touch—whatever it takes—so they can truly understand what is being taught. You have to be creative to get some students' attention, but once you do, you can just feel the enthusiasm and interest blossom.

—THOMAS PAULSEN, *Iowa Teacher of the Year*

I want to be the best I can be, and I want to know as much as I can know. I plant those seeds in my children. I want them to be practical, but I want them to enjoy life, and I want them to know that everything they learn may not come out of their book.

—HARRIET JO BIEHLE, *Kentucky Teacher of the Year*

We not only have to teach our students what is in the textbook, but also how to use the information to become a successful and happy person. We must teach them that it is important to be reliable, trustworthy, and dependable. We must teach them to be hard-working and dedicated.

—SHIRLEY HARRIS, *Teacher of the Year for Louisiana's St. John the Baptist Parish*

Our job is not necessarily to be information givers, it's to draw things out of kids. There aren't easy answers to the best questions. There may not be answers at all. But in throwing them around, we get to learn a lot about ourselves and the subjects.

—DAVID LUSSIER, *Massachusetts Teacher of the Year*

The longer I teach, the more I realize that although we need to teach facts for a basis of thought and discussion, more importantly, we need to teach process and discovery. No longer do I spend hours making up "good" multiple-choice tests. Kids learn through discussion, creating, composing, and connecting. No "perfect test" that I could give would in any way equal the learning that takes place when I ask them to create a question and answer it or discuss an issue and justify their ideas.

—*Minnesota's* MARY BETH BLEGEN,
   National Teacher of the Year

Students must believe that what they are learning is the most important thing they could be doing with their time. I pay close attention to community and world events and attempt to integrate them into our work, whenever possible. Another way to motivate students is to find ways in which the students' work can be recognized and valued. Displays throughout the school, competitions and awards, and finding appropriate audiences are all strategies to give added importance to their work.

—CARYN ELLISON,
   Mishawaka, Indiana, Teacher of the Year

I encourage my students to explore the origins of ideas and materials that have long been buried under a gravestone inscribed, "Taken for Granted." There is nothing like the taste of joy I experience with and through the children as they encounter the fascinations of the world around them.

—STEVEN LEVY, *Massachusetts Teacher of the Year*

I want kids to be careful consumers of what it is that's presented as truth, knowledge. I want them to get the sense that everything they think they know isn't necessarily so.

—DON JOHNSON, *Minnesota Teacher of the Year*

We need to design school programs to prepare children to be lifelong learners. I encourage them to explore and to be flexible.

—CYNTHIA KALKWARF,
Missouri Teacher of the Year

We know how children learn and what we should do in the classroom. If you look, you see it. Skills are being taught and practiced. I give them information they have to take, use, and process. Then it's their knowledge.

—MARSHA JAN DUKE, *California Teacher of the Year*

When I started teaching kids to write, I thought, "If I just correct these mistakes, it doesn't mean anything to these kids." I just found if I could make learning come to life, the children really retained what I was teaching. My vision is to have fully literate people. I see us trying to achieve full literacy, where people read for pleasure, for knowledge.

—Barbara Prentiss,
    New Hampshire Teacher of the Year

I want enlightened skeptics. I don't want students to be patsies for political movements or social movements. I want them to be able to reserve for themselves the right to research something and come to their own conclusions and then have the self-worth to stand on those principles.

—Martin Schmitz,
    Technology & Learning's
    New Mexico Teacher of the Year

Strained relationships in the classroom make learning unpleasant, and may, in fact, produce in students an intense and lasting dislike for education. On the other hand, inspiring students with a sense of their own worth gives them the confidence to express themselves more freely, to explore and learn through their mistakes and to regard learning as an adventure.

—*New York's* JAY SOMMER,
National Teacher of the Year

One of my main goals is to stress in students how important it is to tackle something tough. And then, how good it feels to come through it.

—DON JOHNSON, *Minnesota Teacher of the Year*

Curriculum can become too important and be imposed down from the top in a vacuum. But we need to take the time to find out what kids think and where they want to go, not just make them memorize things because that's what we think they should know.

—CAROL BLEIFIELD, *Wisconsin Teacher of the Year*

Students must do in order to know. Teachers must be given the tools to allow students to create, not just to memorize.

—E. FRANK BLUESTEIN,
Tennessee Teacher of the Year

The first and foremost job of a teacher is to teach kids to think—not just memorize facts and formulas, but to know and understand.

—MIKE BYNUM, *Oklahoma Teacher of the Year*

My goal is active participation. Real learning comes from using the whole mind—seeing, hearing, touching, and smelling.

—*Tennessee's* TERRY WEEKS,
National Teacher of the Year

Teachers have to establish that learning doesn't just take place in the school. It's a lifestyle. In the information age, you have to keep current. Anyone who doesn't, stagnates.

—*Virginia's* PHILIP BIGLER,
National Teacher of the Year

You have to take learning and make it real-life. I do a lot of critical thinking, problem solving, a lot of hands-on, inquiry-based learning. I do things to prepare students for life.

—CHARLES MERCER JR.,
Washington, D.C., Teacher of the Year

If I want the students to be lifelong learners, then I need to be one. If I want them to be diligent and creative in their tasks, then I need to be also. If I want them to work together cooperatively and to be problem solvers, then I need to have that attitude with my colleagues.

> —CARYN ELLISON,
> *Mishawaka, Indiana, Teacher of the Year*

Teachers need to look beyond what they see in the day-to-day outcomes, and look further down the road to what the student might become.

> —PAM CASSAR, *High School Teacher of the Year for Louisiana's St. Bernard Parish*

Watching them learn for the sake of learning is the real joy of this profession. . . . It's not where we start but where we finish that is the important thing.

> —*Alaska's* TERRY JORGENSEN,
> *BP Teacher of Excellence*

Our schools are just empty, impersonal places. It is the students, the teachers, and the principals who bring them to life and give them an identity. For a brief moment in time, these special people create a living, vibrant community of learners dedicated to the universal search for truth and, in Thomas Jefferson's words, "the illimitable freedom of the human mind."

> —*Virginia's* PHILIP BIGLER,
> *National Teacher of the Year*

On the Subjects

My greatest reward is seeing the students' boundless excitement as we move from subject to subject.

—JUNE MOORE, *Wyoming Teacher of the Year*

Kindergarten was all creative and fun. Then came first grade with desks in a row and everyone being asked to do the same thing at the same time. I didn't like that at all and I made a decision then to be a first-grade teacher and to make it fun. . . . Six-year-olds are fascinating people and there is such a wide range of learning styles. Teaching first grade is about understanding the whole child and taking the time to teach them personally.

—DAWN MCNAIR,
Massachusetts Teacher of the Year

I encourage students to relax and let the math happen. I know it's inside them and it's my job to help pull it out—not cram it in!

—*Alaska's* LINDA L. D. SMITH,
BP Teacher of Excellence

It's important to give students a purpose, a goal for learning. You can concentrate just on teaching kids math, and a lot of them will get it. But if you also teach them how to connect with it, how to actually use it, they ultimately learn more from it.

—RAY PINDER,
  Hernando County, Florida, Teacher of the Year

All students can learn more advanced math when they are taught to use real-world problems and manipulatives that make them feel less intimidated by the often-daunting nature of the subject.

—RACHEL NEWMAN-TURNER,
  Maryland Teacher of the Year

There are people who do math and people who like and enjoy math. You have to love it yourself. Math is a tool, but I don't think that's sufficient. It's so much more than seeing two numbers on a piece of paper.

—HELEN BANZHAF, *Nebraska Teacher of the Year*

I can teach my students history facts and multiplication tables, but it is when I see frightened or shy children with low self-esteem become self-confident, stand proud of themselves, fail but have no fear of trying again—laugh at their mistakes and enjoy their successes—that I feel I have truly taught them.

> —*Alaska's* MARGARET PHILLIPS,
> *BP Teacher of Excellence*

My first year of teaching, I realized there was a whole group of students in the classroom that I wasn't hitting. I think the way we teach science is geared toward the left-brain learner—people who are very organized, very analytical, who like numbers and like order. And they tend to be not very creative. Right-brain people are not as organized and are more artsy; they don't typically fit into our educational system as we know it today. I'm left brain; my wife is right brain. So I've tried to change the way I teach. I try to do as many demonstrations as I can. Hands-on science equals hands-on learning.

> —BILL RICHEY, *Ohio Teacher of the Year*

You can learn to be a better person from history. When you've seen what other people faced, you can take heart.

> —*Virginia's* PHILIP BIGLER,
> *National Teacher of the Year*

You never know how you're going to touch kids. They're all special. I was special with my ADD [Attention Deficit Disorder]. They all have something to give. I don't care so much if they know when the Revolutionary War started. If they learn to treat each other with respect and love learning, then I've done my job.

> —CATHY CERVENY, *Maryland Teacher of the Year*

I started off wanting to be a great teacher of history. But now that I've matured, I would rather be respected as a great teacher of students.

> —DAVID LUSSIER,
> *Massachusetts Teacher of the Year*

I tell my students, "If history is boring, then we're boring."

> —ANTHONY J. BERARD, *Anne Arundel County,*
> *Maryland, Teacher of the Year*

My mission is to introduce my students to another culture, not just to teach a language.

> —EMMA E. ISLER,
> *Washington, D.C., Teacher of the Year*

The greatest challenge facing education is getting kids to read. They are bombarded by visuals. That's why teachers need to talk about books all the time and why they're exciting. Books are to a historian what test tubes are to scientists.

—*Virginia's* PHILIP BIGLER,
National Teacher of the Year

We need to do more for early literacy in the classroom and at home. We need to get this message to the parents, the baby sitter, the nanny.

—DAWN MCNAIR,
Massachusetts Teacher of the Year

I make students want to be in the classroom, because no matter what piece of literature I teach, it can speak to them. I tell them, "There are messages in there I can help you to see, and you're going to learn about yourself."

—TALITA DENEGRI, *Oklahoma Teacher of the Year*

By way of writing and literature, I claim as my province the entire range of human experience. What a challenge this is! I offer my students as many ideas as I can by showing them, through literature, that there is nothing that has not already been felt, experienced, or thought, but much to be discovered in a new way.

> —*California's* JANIS T. GABAY,
> *National Teacher of the Year*

Sometimes you look around the class and try to figure out which is the one who will someday be the writer or the journalist or the teacher. You don't always know which are the ones absorbing what you say.

> —HARRIET PAUL JONQUIERE,
> *New York Teacher of the Year*

I make them understand that analyzing a poem or a novel is the same as analyzing a legal brief. It's all about learning how to think.

> —LAURIE COKER,
> *Texas High School English Teacher of the Year*

The moment I waltzed into my first English classroom and spied 27 pairs of eyes, slightly glazed but still conscious enough to wonder what new

methods of torture I was going to devise to bore
them to death, I was hooked on teaching.

—ROBIN D. SMITH, *Virginia Teacher of the Year*

I teach little children to read. I hold the values of
our culture and the history of our world before
them like a sweet confection. I make them reach out
and grab their education from me. I possess the
power to lace their intake with arsenic or sweet
nectar, creating their self-esteem or destroying it. I
shudder under the burden of such a responsibility.

—*West Virginia's* RAE ELLEN MCKEE,
    National Teacher of the Year

First grade is the "A-ha!" year. It's the year when
everything starts and upon which a child builds an
education career. They come in learning to read and
leave reading to learn.

—DAWN MCNAIR,
    Massachusetts Teacher of the Year

The more a student reads and writes, the more
exposure he or she receives in discovering new ideas,
new worlds. Nothing is more rewarding for a

teacher than when a student experiences an epiphany regarding an idea or a concept about life, about learning, about himself. Isn't that what teaching is all about?

—TALITA DENEGRI, *Oklahoma Teacher of the Year*

I don't want to spend every day with a pencil and paper when there are so many other things—dance, music, art—to use.

—LINDA KOSSLER,
Canton, Ohio, Teacher of the Year

Schools need to prepare students for the real world, and to that end we need to give students tools for healthy self-expression and developing emotional intelligence. I believe it's the arts that can do that.

—BRETT SMITH, *Minnesota Teacher of the Year*

Our children need to discover art. Perhaps the war against drugs, alcohol, and violence would be more successful if our children knew how to express themselves better.

—STEVE HORNYAK, *Colorado Teacher of the Year*

The fine arts are seen to be expendable, to be fluff. But I've found over the years that through music and the other arts we are often able to reach students and help them in other academic areas.

—CANDACE BUTLER,
  South Bend, Indiana, Teacher of the Year

I spend a fair amount of time researching the perfect activity that illustrates a concept. For example, when studying the difference between chemical and physical changes, we eat both fizzy candies and Pop Rocks and analyze their ingredients. When learning about light, we examine glow-in-the-dark toys, take apart road flares, and wear rainbow glasses. I strive to create a questioning, problem-solving atmosphere in my classroom that fosters excitement and enthusiasm for science. How can a student not be stimulated when creating a purple gas or seeing a gummy bear go up in flames? What better way to teach freezing point depression than making ice cream? Hopefully, students will come away from my class feeling that science is interesting and available for everyone, not just the nerds of the world.

—BONNIE BUDDENDECK,
  Centerville, Ohio, Teacher of the Year

Teachers teach values whether they do it intentionally or not.

—NANCY TALBOTT, *Kansas Teacher of the Year*

I don't think we should stand up and teach the Ten Commandments. But things like, "Cheating is not right, murder is not right," those are easy. Those are things that nobody should argue against.

—JERRY HOWLAND,
Massachusetts Teacher of the Year

I don't see how I can be value-neutral. If you don't stand up for what you believe in, who's going to stand up for it?

—NINA FUE, *New Jersey Teacher of the Year*

One of the best ways to teach character to kids is to be a good role model. . . . They may not realize it now, but just being here, being an example for them, it's going to influence them. To me, that's worth everything.

—CONNIE RUSSELL, *Cabarrus County,
North Carolina, Teacher of the Year*

It's unrealistic to expect students to be better than their role models. I read somewhere that values are caught as well as taught.

—LINDA BATES, *New Mexico Teacher of the Year*

We have to teach ethical values. In the past we could rely on some general feelings or the word "democracy." Now, we have to be more specific.

—*New York's* JAY SOMMER,
National Teacher of the Year

Challenges in and out of the Classroom

The strengths of America's schools arise from a perceived fault. The positive side of our undisciplined nature is our indomitable spirit. My message to Americans is to glory in the ragged edges of our spontaneous enthusiasm. Don't wish for a unilateral answer to our educational dilemmas. There will never be a single solution that will be a perfect fit for our diverse society. Instead, we should work toward partnerships of families, communities, and educators who enjoy the process of problem solving.

> —*Alaska's* ELAINE GRIFFIN,
>   *National Teacher of the Year*

Beginning teachers are often on probationary contract and given three sink-or-swim classes that no one wants. We've all heard it: "If you're in it for the love of teaching, you'll survive this year." But, in fact, many don't.

> —JEFF JOHNSTON, *Nevada Teacher of the Year*

We know why teachers leave. They don't leave because of the money; surveys tell us they leave because of working conditions. What that usually means is an overwhelming amount of classes, or

huge numbers of students in those classrooms. . . .
I think we're going about it backwards if we try to
raise salaries first. Of course, we must pay for it, but
either we will pay the price through paying teachers
what their training, dedication, and their love
deserves, or our children will pay the price with
their education at the hands of unqualified teachers.
So I think it's very important that we continue to
raise those standards. And teachers want to learn
more; they want to be good.

> —*Vermont's* MICHELE FORMAN,
> *National Teacher of the Year*

Teachers have all the same challenges society has to
contend with, in the classroom. And to keep good
people in the job, it requires a support network.

> —JIM LINSELL, *Michigan Teacher of the Year*

We keep hearing that teachers unions are responsible
for problems in the system, and there's some
credibility for this. Unions have done some bad
things in the interest of keeping teachers in the
system.

> —VALERIE EVANS, *Illinois Teacher of the Year*

If the children can't understand what's happening, teaching isn't going on.

> —REBA MAXSON, *North Carolina's*
> *Region 5 Middle School Teacher of the Year*

In our society where a quality education is a basic prerequisite for success, there can and should be no excuse for poor teachers.

> —*Virginia's* PHILIP BIGLER,
> *National Teacher of the Year*

Our students deserve a world-class education system. We should make sure that every student has a desk, proper supplies, and an air-conditioned space without roof leaks. We have to be able to pay to keep well-qualified teachers. We need good working conditions so students can learn and teachers can teach.

> —VALERIE MAXWELL, *Missouri Teacher of the Year*

I'm really worried about the teacher shortage, and the cause of that, of course, is compensation. It's difficult to attract the best when other jobs simply outbid education.

> —GAIL WORTMANN, *Iowa Teacher of the Year*

Public education cannot be under-funded and still provide viable opportunities for our children and grandchildren.

> —TERRY BEAVER, *Montana Teacher of the Year*

Money buys everything. Money is the answer. Special education costs more. Summer school costs money.

> —LORI UROGDY EILER, *Ohio Teacher of the Year*

It was really hard for me to accept the fact that I'd been laid off when I work so hard. But in truth, many good teachers are laid off. I used to say it's unbelievable. Now I say it's all too believable.

> —CATHY NELSON,
> *Minnesota Teacher of the Year,*
> *on being laid off four times during budget crises*

It's important that students don't use their poverty or bad home situations as excuses for failure. I believe everyone has a gift to develop and pursue as a career. My gift is teaching.

> —MARY LOSTETTER,
> *South Carolina Teacher of the Year*

I can't do anything about what happens the other 23 hours and 15 minutes. Some of these kids know more about how to get the utilities turned back on and when the payments come from the state than I will ever know. There are some days that are so sad I think I'd rather flip burgers for a while than do this anymore.

—DIANE CRIM,
   Utah Teacher of the Year

When students who have grown up with satellites, computers, air conditioning, and heart transplants turn into the voting populace, it is little wonder that it takes bigger and more fascinating issues than faculty renovation or "paper and pencil" money to gain their tax dollars.

—*West Virginia's* RAE ELLEN MCKEE,
   National Teacher of the Year

Kids in inner cities deserve the same equitable education as kids in the upper classes of society. OK, maybe their language is horrible, maybe their behavior needs some help, but I can still teach them. I don't just teach math, science, and history. I teach life: How to communicate with one another; how to end a conflict in a peaceful manner; how to get what you need without taking it.

—*California's* SANDRA MCBRAYER,
National Teacher of the Year

The rule is: The poorer the children, the poorer the educational system. Not because we don't care about them—we care deeply about them—but look at the buildings, look at the class sizes, the teachers are overwhelmed with 35, 40 kids whose needs are enormous. It burns teachers right up. They're human beings, they love these kids, but they get out because they have to survive. They're crashing. They have no way they can begin to meet the needs of these children. The turnover in poor urban schools and poor rural areas is disgraceful. You get the least-qualified teachers—fresh with no experience, or people who are burned out at the other end—and we have to change that.

—*Vermont's* MICHELE FORMAN,
National Teacher of the Year

Research shows kids learn better in smaller classrooms. You are able to do more, reach them, be more creative. That is so important. In most countries doing well with students academically, you have small classes.

—HENRY BROWN III,
Florida Teacher of the Year

We need to re-examine the environment we create in large schools. . . . We need to work harder making schools smaller—if not physically smaller, then smaller classes and smaller environments at big schools. We need to emphasize that schools are communities and we have mutual obligations to each other. Too many people see schools as places where kids pass through. The concept of a school within a school has been around for a long time. We emphasize big athletics that involve a relatively small number of kids vs. other programs that involve a lot of kids. There are some things from an educational view that may not seem that important but from a community point of view may be very important, like clubs and special events like homecoming or school fairs—whatever that school does to make kids feel part of the community. The same principles that create a better town and city should be true in a school.

—MARK MAVROGIANES,
Colorado Teacher of the Year

There is no one test that should define the rest of one's life, just like no college should go only on SATs. But I believe standardized tests have a place in the larger educational assessment picture.

> —MARIANNE MORAN,
> *Massachusetts Teacher of the Year*

When we find ourselves paralyzed by the rhetoric of accountability, high-stakes testing, and performance-based standards, we must remember our most fundamental mission—to help students learn better.

> —CHRISTA M. COMPTON,
> *South Carolina Teacher of the Year*

The emphasis on high-stakes, multiple-choice testing is destructive. It's gone too far. It's eating up too much of our resources. Mandating grades 3 through 8 testing is of very dubious value. It's of no value to teachers because it's not diagnostic. All it does is artificially spread out scores and rank kids. It doesn't tell me what my students can do and cannot do. It soaks up enormous resources. Not just money, but time, focus, attention. It can point to something a student does know, but no multiple-choice test can tell me what a student does not know. There are too many reasons why we do poorly on multiple-choice tests. They also lead us to the weakest kind of teaching, that is for surface memorization, rather than deep thinking and learning.

—*Vermont's* MICHELE FORMAN,
   National Teacher of the Year

We must put our curriculums on the table and ask frightening and challenging questions such as, "What are the kids learning from that material?" Perhaps even more frightening is what comes after the questions are asked. We are here to help students develop skills which will carry them into another century which promises to be no less revolutionary than the Industrial Revolution of the late 18th and early 19th centuries. A century which promises excitement and frustration with the explosion of technology.

—*Minnesota's* MARY BETH BLEGEN,
   National Teacher of the Year

I don't worry about meeting someone else's standards in my classroom. I have standards.

—*North Carolina's* JAMES ROGERS,
   National Teacher of the Year

I would encourage teachers to take an active part in the political processes that govern our schools and to resist the temptation to confine themselves to the four walls of their classrooms. There has never been a time when teacher voice and teacher activism were more needed or more important than they are right now.

—*Georgia's* ANDY BAUMGARTNER,
National Teacher of the Year

I've seen the teaching profession honored and yet not listened to. I hope I have spread the message that all education takes place in the classroom and any reform movement must begin with the teachers in the classroom.

—MARIANNE MORAN,
Massachusetts Teacher of the Year

Educators are the best experts at solving education problems. Their solutions need to be supported. They need more time in the classroom and more money spent in the classroom to achieve goals.

—KATHERINE KOCH-LAVEEN,
Minnesota Teacher of the Year

Teachers are not given enough flexibility or allowed
enough participation in decision-making to have
their expertise work for them. There are some
things a principal or a superintendent cannot know
about a classroom. They know a lot, but there are
things that only somebody on the front line knows.
In the Persian Gulf war, for instance, you didn't see
Colin Powell going out with weapons the way his
soldiers did. He knew where his place was. Powell
depended on his soldiers to help him decide the next
move because they were out there seeing what was
going on. I see this as an analogy to teachers. We
know what works and doesn't work from our
experience. We need to be given a chance to speak,
to make decisions, to help plan what our schools are
going to be like. That also brings accountability and
a deeper commitment.

—ANNIE PEGRAM,
North Carolina Teacher of the Year

Among our biggest challenges in education today is
improving our public image. So much has been
written in recent years on what is wrong with
education; we need to do a better job of focusing
public attention on our accomplishments. Every
school and every school district across the nation

needs to formalize an aggressive public information system to carry the positive message of even our small victories to the public on a regular basis.

—*Virginia's* MARY V. BICOUVARIS,
National Teacher of the Year

We must restore teaching to its rightful status as a profession. We must give our teachers the respect and support they need to accomplish the awesome mission they have been given. For too long, we have taken for granted their dedication and hard work. We have given them greater and greater responsibilities and thanked them less and less.

—*South Carolina's* TERRY KNECHT DOZIER,
National Teacher of the Year

The ills of society happen to be knocking at the schoolhouse doors. We seem to be surprised that issues of poverty, homelessness, drug abuse, teen pregnancy, and teen suicide are coming to our school campuses, and we're looking at one set of people, who happen to be educators, for a solution. I'm not letting the community off the hook.

—*California's* SANDRA MCBRAYER,
National Teacher of the Year

There has been a change in students as far as their home life. A lot of them come from broken homes and they spend part of the time with their mother and part of the time with their father and they have a hard time knowing about authority, who is in charge.

—LOIS COOPER FREEMAN,
Arkansas Teacher of the Year

Schools have always served two different roles: they are the guardians of traditional values, but they also have a responsibility to be innovative and respond to the problems of the times. And one of the problems of the times is AIDS. There are issues that, like it or not, you have to deal with. Lots of us might complain about that. It would be nice and simple if this were a Dick and Jane world, and Spot and Puff were running around in a nice little suburban world, but it's not that way anymore. It's not that way in suburbia, either.

—FRANK D. GAWLE, *Connecticut Teacher of the Year*

It's not technology that's really changed teaching. It's the continuous breakdown of family.

—JOHN MANUSZAK,
Mishawaka, Indiana, Teacher of the Year

I don't think kids get talked to at home. Teachers have been talking about how kids are noisier, but some of us were talking the other day and said, "You know, when else do kids get a chance to talk or be listened to?" We need to be partners in education, and parents have to help.

—BARBARA PRENTISS,
New Hampshire Teacher of the Year

There are a lot more broken homes, a lot more dual parents, where the child will spend one week with one parent and the next with the other. It is a trend, and you have to take that into consideration with some children. I try to instill built-in standards of performance and feelings of pride in achievement. I use every opportunity to build an understanding and communication between the child and myself.

—MARJORIE DRAHOS,
New Jersey Teacher of the Year

These days, I don't think you can separate home from school. If the 7th-grader is abusing drugs, he can't put that down when he comes to school. If the teenage girl is pregnant, she can't cover it up and leave it at home. If the first-grade child is being neglected and abused at home, that is going to show up somehow at school. For years, we have looked at parents being our aides, our assistants, but nowadays with all the problems that we have, we need to be aides of the parents.

> —ANNIE PEGRAM,
> *North Carolina Teacher of the Year*

Where it is always appropriate to hold teachers accountable for doing their job, which is teaching, it is not always possible to hold them responsible for doing the student's job, which is learning. A student's ability to learn is influenced by too many factors outside the teacher's realm: his innate ability, his environment, his family's support, his peer involvement, and his reactions to the messages of society.

> —*West Virginia's* RAE ELLEN MCKEE,
> *National Teacher of the Year*

There are so many things children have to deal with out in the real world that I feel like my job is to make them feel safe while they're here. . . . They help run the classroom and that way the classroom belongs to them.

> —CATHY PIHL, *Tennessee Teacher of the Year*

If the adult population in our country were asked about its most difficult issues, I believe communication problems with spouse, family, or co-workers; problems with personal finance; and child rearing would top the list. Education must give all students opportunities to learn skills for resolving conflicts; identifying and constructively dealing with personal feelings; parenting; and personal financial management.

—P. BRETT SMITH,
Minnesota Teacher of the Year

I worry so much about what I read about kids in trouble and bad decisions they make. It makes me realize kids need to think critically. There won't always be someone there to hold their hand. Eventually, they'll be running the show.

—PAT ROSSMAN, *Wisconsin Teacher of the Year*

An old proverb asserts that "Civilization begins anew with each child." As an educator, I have found this statement to be both a vision of optimism as well as a dire warning. On one hand, our students are the intellectual heirs to Plato, Aristotle, Augustine, and Newton; the inheritors of a rich

legacy of human progress traversing three millennia.
Conversely, if we fail to successfully teach and
educate our young people, we are just one
generation removed from barbarism.

> —*Virginia's* PHILIP BIGLER,
> *National Teacher of the Year*

The real teachers of the year are those who report to
school each day despite physical threats to their
safety; or teachers who don't lose their enthusiasm
for teaching even when they're surrounded by tired
and pessimistic colleagues. It is to these teachers, and
the many others who succeed despite the odds, for
whom I take off my hat and to whom each of us
owes a vote of gratitude.

> —*Georgia's* ANDY BAUMGARTNER,
> *National Teacher of the Year*

There are some kids who have a strong fear about
school. I don't share that. Random acts of madness
can happen anywhere on any given day. . . . I know
school violence has increased. But on the day of
Columbine, a whole bunch of kids, 30 to 45 million,
went to school, and nothing bad happened to them.
If I stop feeling safe and start looking at kids with
suspicion, my effectiveness as an educator is

dramatically compromised. You go into a trial with a presumption of innocence, and you go into the classroom with a presumption of trust. I trust my kids and I feel safe in my school. I feel very bad about those people who don't.

—MARK MAVROGIANES,
Colorado Teacher of the Year

It is very easy to become disillusioned from all that we hear outside of education itself. It feels like oftentimes we are not supported. We're not acknowledged. We're seen as those people who do those tasks, rather than as professionals. That disappoints me and personally even affected me at one point where I really stopped to reconsider whether I was in the right profession. But I'm very optimistic about education. I cannot be a teacher without being an optimist. I have great faith in the abilities of our students. That's my job, to tap that, to elicit that, to bring out that performance. Every student is full of marvelous potential.

—*California's* JANIS T. GABAY,
National Teacher of the Year

It makes me feel old to see students come back to visit and they're all grown up. At the school, we pretty much stay the same, but the kids are always growing.

—LOURDES CASCIARI, *Teacher of the Year at
Florida's Sebastian Elementary*

I wish teachers were respected according to their contribution to society.

—CYNTHIA KALKWARF,
Missouri Teacher of the Year

I want to celebrate us as teachers. I want to celebrate us as givers of hope to classrooms full of children across this country. We are the ones who listen to kids. I want to challenge us to do more and do it better. Today's kids deserve change in schools and particularly in classrooms. Today's kids deserve to be taught how to think, how to process, and how to analyze. They learn when they are emotionally engaged in what they are doing.

—*Minnesota's* MARY BETH BLEGEN,
National Teacher of the Year

All too often, schools get knocked down, they get a bad rap. Here's a mystery: Somehow, if we have a bad primary education system, why is it that we have what is universally recognized as the finest higher education system in the world? Does something magically happen between June and September, when they enroll in college? Of course not. People come from all over the world to attend American universities.

> —*Vermont's* MICHELE FORMAN,
> *National Teacher of the Year*

As educators, we do have a lot of challenges and a lot of work ahead of us, but I think it's going to be an exciting future.

> —DAVID LUSSIER,
> *Massachusetts Teacher of the Year*

Leaving No
Child Behind

We must save at-risk students today or fear them tomorrow.

—HENRY BROWN III,
Florida Teacher of the Year

Eighty-five percent of all prison inmates are high-school dropouts. That tells you right there that if we can get them through high school, they have a chance.

—*California's* SANDRA MCBRAYER,
National Teacher of the Year

Classes should be an adventure every day. They should be places where children discover, where failure is kept at bay. When a school fails a child, it fails an entire family.

—*Georgia's* ANDY BAUMGARTNER,
National Teacher of the Year

I teach students how to be risk-takers, to not be afraid to take chances or try something new—that failure is a part of life, something we have to learn.

—CAROLE FIRESTONE,
California Teacher of the Year

How many students wake up saying, "Yay, today I'm going to fail!" I tell students that if they didn't make that affirmation this morning in the shower, they better not make it in my classroom. . . . I tell them, "Everyone is going to be successful, bottom line, period. That is not up for discussion. Now, how are you going to get there?"

—DEBORAH JOHNSTON,
Colorado Teacher of the Year

My motto for kids is, "Your best will do just fine."

—ANNMARIE WRIGHT,
Jenks, Oklahoma, Teacher of the Year

I always say give me the underdog—that's who I want. They know what it's like to struggle. And when they do taste success, it's a sweet success. They have to taste success. If they haven't tasted it, they don't know what they are missing.

—XOCHITL FUHRIMAN-EBERT,
Oregon Teacher of the Year

I never considered my teaching to be exceptional. It's just what I do. I wanted to reach the kids who were falling through the cracks, who weren't reaching their potential in a structure of the traditional sort.

—MOLLY MERRY, *Colorado Teacher of the Year*

I believe all children can learn, no matter what. I tell people not to live off excuses, put your best foot forward and be respectful. No matter what the circumstance, you are able to learn and do your best.

—CHARLES MERCER JR.,
Washington, D.C., Teacher of the Year

One thing I've learned is that special education cannot be isolated from regular education. Together, we all make the difference.

—PATRICIA BRINDLEY,
South Bend, Indiana, Teacher of the Year

I've found when you mainstream special-needs students with regular kids it's the typical students who gain the most. Most people expect it to be the reverse.

—KRIS DOSAL, *Teacher of the Year at
Tampa, Florida's Grady Elementary*

What's best for the best is best for the rest. I teach students of all levels with the same goal in mind.

—DEBORAH SHEPARD, *Teacher of the Year at Leon County, Florida's Lincoln High*

I see the abilities in my students rather than the disabilities in them. I treat my students as capable learners and will do whatever it takes to motivate them to learn. I let my students know that I am happy to see them at school. Maybe my good-morning smile will help them to feel special, too.

—JANET FREAD, *Teacher of the Year for Louisiana's St. John the Baptist Parish*

Education is about helping others understand how valuable they are to the functioning of the whole. I approach every one of my students with the thought, "How are you smart?" rather than "How smart are you?"

—JEFFREY LUKENS, *South Dakota Teacher of the Year*

Everybody deserves an education based on their ability. Of course you're always going to have kids who don't attend or don't want to attend; after you give them a bunch of chances, finally you say one day, "OK, John or Mary, this isn't working so I'm going to try to guide you toward a GED or adult basic education." That's fine. But for kids who want to be in school—who come and try—they should be able to be educated toward their ability, not to what legislation has decided they need to learn or know.

—JIM DUERST,
Sarasota County, Florida, Teacher of the Year

I really look at each child individually to see what I can do to make each child succeed. With both parents working and with different family arrangements, I think schools are going to have to be more innovative.

—MARGARET A. DUNCAN,
Idaho Teacher of the Year

I don't think there's a child that can't learn. I want to take every child I've got as far as they can go. As far back as I can remember, I have been teaching. Once something had been learned, I had to pass it along to someone else whether they seemed willing or not.

—JO CROW, *Illinois Teacher of the Year*

I encourage teachers and the general public to cast off any preconceived notions they may have about the ability of children from different cultural backgrounds to succeed academically. All children can and will learn in an environment that values individual differences and fosters a life-long love of learning. If we ever plan to close the achievement gap between different socioeconomic and ethnic groups, we must all raise our expectations and demand that others do the same. Educators must work together to dispel the myth that children from low-income backgrounds and those from racial and language minority groups cannot succeed. They can.

—TRACY CALLARD, *Kansas Teacher of the Year*

My goal is to make a difference in every student's life. I know that we only have them for a little time, but while they're in my presence, I would like to be able to open an eye for them to see that they can cultivate a dream. I try to empower my students to believe in their gifts, their talent, and their ability. There is no excuse to not succeed or be the very best that you can be.

—CONSTANCE JORDAN,
  Wal-Mart/Sam's Club
  Kentucky Teacher of the Year

We have to be able to see and recognize the genius in each child. It's not always academic, but it's there. I like to give each child an opportunity in the course of the year to shine before their fellow students, to express the gift that God has planted in them.

—STEVEN LEVY, *Massachusetts Teacher of the Year*

If a student has self-esteem and believes in his inherent value and goodness as a human being, then he will learn; he will not allow himself to fail.

—BYRON KELIM,
Hazelwood, Missouri, Teacher of the Year

I make sure my students know that I am a human being who cares if they attend my class, who cares that they work to their potential, who cares that they show respect for themselves and others. I let students know that it is all right to make mistakes, as long as they adjust and learn from their mistakes.

—MARIANNE MACCARTHY TRUE,
New Hampshire Teacher of the Year

I teach to give voice to those often left unheard. I teach to spark imaginations. I teach for probing questions that challenge the status quo. Being a teacher is far beyond a career to me; it is the essence of who I am—for I see our nation's future in the eyes of my students. I teach to touch that future.

—Barbara LaSaracina,
   New Jersey Teacher of the Year

I see my role as a facilitator of learning. I try to make it possible for all my students to have a chance to be successful at tasks that suit their talents and to see that someone loves them and cares about what they accomplish. I personally invite all my students to become active participants in their own learning.

—*Ohio's* Bruce Brombacher,
   National Teacher of the Year

I do not accept "I can't." I will only accept "I will try."

—Bonnie McNeill,
   Aiken County, South Carolina, Teacher of the Year

I want the same things, basically, for my students that I want for my own children. I want them to be kind. I want them to be fair to people, to care about people. They need to be able to take care of themselves and to be committed somehow to taking care of others, whether their community or their country, but to have a commitment to something, to a set of ideals. I want them never to settle for less than their best. That's a lot isn't it? I want them to be the best they can be.

—MAUREEN WHELAN SPAIGHT,
Rhode Island Teacher of the Year

All students can and should learn. I have come to believe in an educational system where excellence is expected and quality is the norm. Otherwise, we are in peril of creating an intellectual caste system with an ever-widening chasm between the educated and uneducated.

—*Virginia's* PHILIP BIGLER,
National Teacher of the Year

My dedication to this school is reinforced by my desire to change lives. Through the years, many of my students have stood at the fork in the road, and it has been my job to guide them to the high road. I believe it is my calling to educate, uplift, and enrich the lives of children with hope and direction.

—CLAUDIA HARRIS, *Spring Branch, Texas,*
Secondary Teacher of the Year

I just expect each student to do their best, no matter what that might be. Special-needs students give you that because they want that praise like other students do.

> —JACK BROCKETTE, *Texas Council of Administrators of Special Education Regular Teacher of the Year*

I would not be here if I did not believe that each and every one of them would be successful in life. Maybe a student's not going to college, but he can be successful at what he does. . . . They need someone who cares. They need someone who's there that they trust.

> —BERNICE WHITE-MORTON, *Newport News, Virginia, Teacher of the Year*

Exceptional teachers imagine the best possibilities in their students rather than crippling them with negative assumptions about what they are or are not capable of doing.

> —PAMELA J. SIMPSON, *Aiken County, South Carolina, Teacher of the Year*

The biggest thing we can do for kids is to teach them to be responsible for themselves because se is going to be responsible for them. I tell my students, "You are perfectly free not to do something. But you have to accept the consequences." I say to them, "I trust everything you tell me until you lie to me. Then I don't believe anything." If you can't be trusted for your word, something's wrong.

—NINA FUE,
New Jersey Teacher of the Year

I hear teachers say that students have the right to fail, and I suppose that's true. But it shouldn't be easy. I am convinced that the vast majority of students, given sufficient time and appropriate types of help, can achieve a level of mastery in any subject area.

—*Virginia's* MARY V. BICOUVARIS,
National Teacher of the Year

All children are creative and talented. There is something special and unique in every one of them. Once I have discovered a child's strength, teaching the subject matter becomes easy.

—KATHRYN MCFARLAND,
Washington Teacher of the Year

Too many teachers treat kids as a number and not a person. It's important to be open and honest with them. And to be a good listener.

> —*Washington's* CHUCK FILIPPINI,
>   *National Traffic Safety Education*
>   *Teacher of the Year*

We, as teachers, have an obligation to help every child in our classes achieve to the highest pinnacle they can. Believing that every child can learn and always entering the classroom with a positive attitude are two qualities every teacher should possess.

> —DANNY PRADO,
>   *West Virginia Teacher of the Year*

A teacher must give extra time to those students who need it.

> —*New York's* JAY SOMMER,
>   *National Teacher of the Year*

I possess a strong desire to work as a teacher and serve as a role model for all children, but particularly for those students who contend with obstacles and cultural deprivation in their daily lives. I have set a personal commitment for myself to become instrumental in helping children succeed in achieving a high degree of determination, noteworthy aspirations, and self-fulfillment. I know that when I teach today, I teach tomorrow.

—SHIRLEY FOLSOM,
  Fairfax County, Virginia, Teacher of the Year

I tell my students the quote I live by daily: "Failure is just a temporary condition." While there is life, there is hope.

—HENRY BROWN III, *Florida Teacher of the Year*

The late Shel Silverstein said, "Listen to the MUSTN'TS, child/Listen to the DON'TS/Listen to the SHOULDN'TS/Listen to the NEVER HAVES/Then listen close to me/Anything can happen, child/ANYTHING can be." It is easy to love children in general, and it is easy to love almost all children individually. Once in a great while there is a child who is difficult to love. It takes a compassionate heart. To ensure that the limitations of the negative "don'ts" and "never haves" are erased from every child's learning experience, a teacher needs to cultivate a mule-headed determination. Determination demands that every child will learn. These two, compassion and determination, are my guidelines as I work with every child every day.

—JEAN PARMER, *Plano, Texas, Secondary Teacher*

Some teachers feel their students cannot learn. No teaching can go on unless you believe your students can do anything. Those teachers have to be recharged, retrained, and re-educated.

—*California's* MARILYN JACHETTI WHIRRY, *National Teacher of the Year*

You can't let anyone down. It's not in the job description.

—JOSEPH BALCHUNAS, *Florida Teacher of the Year*

In my class, every student is considered gifted. I try to praise their strong areas and gently work with them to improve the weak areas of learning. I spend many hours on boosting self-esteem. One great reward from this is that they boost my self-esteem.

—LOIS COOPER FREEMAN, *Arkansas Teacher of the Year*

Every day I stand at the classroom door and hug
children who maybe others are afraid of hugging or
don't want to hug and we do not judge. Everyone
who walks in the door, no matter what they look
like, no matter what they're wearing or what they
smell like, we hug them; we care for them; we
believe in their potential.

> —*California's* SANDRA MCBRAYER,
> *National Teacher of the Year,*
> *on working at a school for homeless children*

Never give up on a child. There are reasons why
children act up that we don't know about. You never
know what a child will become.

> —HENRY BROWN III, *Florida Teacher of the Year*

I believe that all students can succeed and that
"at-risk" students are really students "at-promise."
They are waiting to bloom. They are crying out for
support. Often they can achieve at high levels when
given the right environment. I was born to become
a teacher, but teaching the "at-promise" students is
what I live for.

> —*Washington's* SHANNON ESPINOZA,
> *Disney American Teacher Award Honoree*

It's the teacher who opens up the door of the world to the kids—takes the questions they have and helps them find answers. The more you expect from a child, the more they will do.

—SUZANNE LULL,
   New Hampshire Teacher of the Year

If a student scores only a 60 on an assignment, I don't pound failure into his head. I tell him, "OK, you've mastered 60 percent of the material. Now let's focus on that 40 percent that you're not grasping." It gives the students another way of measuring their success so they don't give up on themselves or on the subject.

—LORRAINE R. MANEEN,
   Texas Secondary Teacher of the Year

I strongly believe that what young people think, say, and write are all significant.

—JO ANN SNYDER HARMAN,
   West Virginia Teacher of the Year

Children know that I really and truly love them. They know that. . . . If one thing doesn't work with a child, you have to find another way. And you

always have to keep their dignity. They know
nobody's going to laugh at them here if they make a
mistake. This is the place we make mistakes.

—RHODA STROUD, *Minnesota Teacher of the Year*

I know that I can't reach 100 percent of my students,
but I feel that I can reach a lot of them. The best
thing to me about being a teacher is being able to
motivate and encourage those kids who might have
a hard time with their lessons.

—DIANN MEEKS,
Glynn County, Florida, Teacher of the Year

Reaching every kid—that's the thing I haven't done
yet. That's my goal. It has to bother you. Otherwise,
you're not doing your job.

—ELIZABETH WINEBARGER,
Hampton City, Virginia, Teacher of the Year

My hardest years were when I was in middle school.
I almost flunked. . . . It was in the sixth grade that I
was reminded I was a failure. The teacher who tried
to tell me I was a negative, I ended up teaching
beside her years later. You can never sum up what a

child will be like. As educators we have to accept that. All children have potential.

> —PENNY FOYE,
>   *Horry County, South Carolina, Teacher of the Year*

I wouldn't have wanted me for a student. I had a big mouth, I hated school, and I was always in trouble. Nobody tried to find out what made me tick except for one person—an English teacher.

> —LAURIE COKER,
>   *Texas High School English Teacher of the Year*

Parents and
Other Partners

The best learning takes place in the context of community.

—CHRISTA M. COMPTON,
    South Carolina Teacher of the Year

If you make students feel the school is theirs, then they're going to protect it. Make them feel it's their community, and they care about it. We yearn for a sense of community whether we live in rural Alaska or New York City.

—*Alaska's* ELAINE GRIFFIN,
    National Teacher of the Year

Teaching and learning form a partnership. They are given and received simultaneously. If I listen carefully to my students, they will give me all the cues I need to teach. Their interests, personalities, and backgrounds provide the foundation for my work. My mission is to be a dream maker for my students, not a dream breaker.

—*California's* CHAUNCEY VEATCH,
    National Teacher of the Year

There are so many things that parents can do so that children come to school prepared to learn. If parents are not supporting their children, it has to be one of two reasons: They either don't know how to support their children, or they don't understand the importance of their support.

> —MARY MORELAND,
> *Muscogee County, Ohio, Teacher of the Year*

The teaching profession is a partnership between the school and home. My journey of learning began with my first two teachers, my parents.

> —MAUREEN HOFFMANN,
> *Iowa Teacher of the Year*

I really want every child to succeed. Sometimes that means taking action outside the classroom, calling on the parents at home.

> —JOAN KNISS,
> *Colorado Teacher of the Year*

I not only call home for negative things but for positive things. The children get a real kick out of that.

> —LARRY BROWN,
> *Washington, D.C., Teacher of the Year*

Parents need to hear the good things about their children. I don't like to call parents only when there is a problem. In order to sustain that, I call throughout the year. It's a 10-minute call that really emphasizes the positive things the student does, rather than a two-hour conference in the spring when the student is failing.

—MARIANNE MACCARTHY TRUE,
New Hampshire Teacher of the Year

My students and their parents can count on my support. Every year I place 450 phone calls or more to students and parents. These connections are intended to outline my program and its goals. Communication, either by phone or during a conference, serves to uplift and support parent and student needs.

—LESLIE REVIS,
South Carolina Teacher of the Year

There are a lot of times that parents need to talk as much as children do.

—ANNIE PEGRAM,
North Carolina Teacher of the Year

With many parents, as long as Mary and Johnny are getting picked up on the bus, school's wonderful. More parents need to realize what their job is, and forget about trying to figure out what makes them happy in their lives.

—JIM DUERST,
    Sarasota County, Florida, Teacher of the Year

Kids like to see parents come to school. Then they see it is important. It is a simple thing, but it really makes a difference in children's attitudes toward school.

—KATHLEEN LOONEY, *Teacher of the Year at Washington Township, Pennsylvania's Grenloch Terrace Early Childhood Center*

It is my fundamental belief that parents perform an act of faith in myself and the school every time they send their child to school. I only capitalize on the already established love, care, and concern parents have for their child when working cooperatively with families throughout the school year.

—*Alaska's* DONI CHICARELL,
    BP Teacher of Excellence

Most parents still do value learning. As a parent myself I think we want the most for our children. We want them to have more than what we had ourselves. We want it to come easier for them and I think that, in wanting to do a lot for our kids, we do too much sometimes. We don't expect them to do enough on their own. It's easier to look for a quick fix than to build the long-term skills they will need. So whether it's expedient for us or whether it's out of love and concern, in wanting to be a good parent, we sometimes do things they should be able to do for themselves.

—MAUREEN WHELAN SPAIGHT,
    Rhode Island Teacher of the Year

Whatever people want for their kids, I want them to work towards that, but I also want them to take the next step and say, "OK, I want my neighbors' kids to have the same chance."

—*California's* SANDRA MCBRAYER,
    National Teacher of the Year

Parents want to get more involved, teachers desperately want more help—but there's a gap between them right now. And we've got to reach out and end that. Everybody I know wants a good life for their kids, no matter how many problems they have themselves. The teacher's role is to say, "I'll work with you to help make that possible." But then the teacher also says to the parent, "You have to help. If your child complains they have too much homework, or we're making them work too hard, don't just badmouth the school. Come and help us improve it."

> —*Alaska's* ELAINE GRIFFIN,
> *National Teacher of the Year*

Parents want to know how you as a teacher deal with children as far as their social growth and development; how you handle behavior problems; and how you actually just talk to the children. Most parents, I think, want somebody who can be firm but fair.

> —ANNIE PEGRAM,
> *North Carolina Teacher of the Year*

We talk about the African proverb: "It takes a village to raise a child." In today's society, many of these kids don't have parents, so other people have to take on the responsibility to treat them as if they were their own children.

—HENRY BROWN III, *Florida Teacher of the Year*

The school must once again be a central focus in each neighborhood, linking teachers, parents, and community to make a difference in the lives of our nation's children, our nation's future contributing citizens.

—*California's* JANIS T. GABAY, *National Teacher of the Year*

I would like to convey to my profession and to the general public my belief that the survival of effective public education is essential to all of us as individuals and a global society. Our future attends school today.

—MARY WILSON EAGER, *Georgia Teacher of the Year*

The goal is to connect with the students and their parents. That way, we have a working relationship and the learning is meaningful, ongoing, and fun.

—MARY ALLAN, *California Teacher of the Year*

Any time you bring the community into the school, or you bring the school out to the community, good things happen.

— CATHY BISSOONDIAL, *Illinois Teacher of the Year*

All educators must be able to answer the student who asks, "Why do I need to know this?" If teachers can create relationships or partnerships with the community, they will be able to answer this question.

— THOMAS PAULSEN, *Iowa Teacher of the Year*

The general public doesn't know a lot of what goes on with teaching, and I would invite them to come to school and become involved—the more the merrier.

— BRIAN RADCLIFFE, *Fayette County, Kentucky, High School Teacher of the Year*

Teaching should be child-centered with a flexible curriculum designed to adequately prepare students to become global citizens in the 21st century. Teaching is a shared responsibility with the school system, the family, the place of worship, and many other community agencies playing a crucial role in the development of the whole child.

—SHERYL ABSHIRE, *Louisiana Teacher of the Year*

The teaching profession cannot exist or succeed in isolation, and the best teacher cannot succeed without the accountability and responsibility of every member of the community.

—*Michigan's* THOMAS A. FLEMING,
National Teacher of the Year

My classroom functions not only as a collection of individuals, but also as a community. Building a sense of community in a relaxed nurturing environment, but in an environment where expectations are high for everyone, is one way to enhance learning, given that most students perform better when they feel secure and important in our group.

—RITA WIGFIELD, *Minnesota Teacher of the Year*

The interaction between the teacher, students, and community members is of paramount importance in teaching and learning. A teacher who knows the community in which he works possesses a better understanding of his job and of his students. It is, therefore, very important that the teacher becomes involved in the life of the community.

> —*New York's* JAY SOMMER,
> *National Teacher of the Year*

It's a team effort. The children I get each year were taught by other teachers, and they've done a fine job in preparing them.

> —MARJORIE DRAHOS,
> *New Jersey Teacher of the Year*

Sometimes people forget how important a job teaching is. My goal is to involve the community and parents as well as students and teachers to raise the standards of education as well as its image.

> —SANDRA HOUK JAMES,
> *Louisiana Teacher of the Year*

The success or demise of the public school system is the responsibility of all members of the public. We have traditionally blamed poor schools on poor teaching and poor teachers and have attempted to pull support from these schools in one way or another. When this happens, everyone suffers a great loss. We must accept the realization that, for all the rhetoric, we have not placed America's children as our nation's first priority. Our policymakers have made excuses for not building the schools we want for our children but have not accepted any responsibility for the results. Most importantly, discussions about improving our schools and upgrading teacher accountability and student achievement too often lack sufficient, if any, input by teachers.

>—*Georgia's* ANDY BAUMGARTNER,
>   *National Teacher of the Year*

Teachers need to be held more accountable for the steady progress of each student. Teachers need to invite other teachers, parents, and resource people to be a part of their classes.

>—MAUREEN HOFFMANN, *Iowa Teacher of the Year*

Only when parents, educators, and students accept their responsibilities will we not only meet standards but we'll exceed them.

>—TANYA N. MARCINKEWICZ,
>   *Delaware Teacher of the Year*

Education is a human relationship based on mutual respect among teachers, students, and community. Every student, regardless of ability, background, or educational objectives, has the right to learn in an atmosphere that is free from fear and prejudice, and is thereby conducive to learning. Perhaps more than anyone else, the teacher has the responsibility to create such an atmosphere. Effective teachers nevertheless realize that any success is superficial if achieved at the expense of fairness. Teachers must treat all students in a consistent and equitable manner.

—*North Carolina's* DONNA H. OLIVER, *National Teacher of the Year*

Education needs to be valued. It needs to be a partnership between parents, teachers, and students. We all have to work together.

—LUCY VENNEN, *Louisiana Teacher of the Year*

Teachers are able to do what they do because they receive support, care, and encouragement from their families, both their families at home and their family of teachers in the school building. I so much appreciate what both families have done for me, and what they do for my colleagues.

—SUSAN MCLEMORE, *Putnam City, Oklahoma,*
Teacher of the Year

We need community support. Without collaboration of all parties, parents, teachers, community members, policymakers, we can't get the job done. It takes all of us working together to make it successful.

—DODIE BURNS MAGILL,
South Carolina Teacher of the Year

When teachers, parents, students, and administrators work together to meet challenges at the local level, the door to excellence is open to all. The size of the community or school is immaterial.

—*Alaska's* ELAINE GRIFFIN,
National Teacher of the Year

As important as academic achievement is—I'm not diminishing that one bit—it should never be allowed to take away from the human characteristic of schools. But a principal that has a choice of working on test scores that will be published in the newspaper April 1 vs. a stronger, healthier school community that in two or three years may pay off. Well, it takes a strong, brave principal to do it. Community building is a far more abstract concept, and it's hard to show those results to the school board or the press or the taxpayer when there's a bond election.

—MARK MAVROGIANES,
Colorado Teacher of the Year

We need an education for everybody, a public awareness, public service announcements, a partnership and a teamwork amongst parents, neighborhood leaders, and school officials to get together and invest in our future, starting from the top; a war on the negatives and a positive war in favor of education, where we invest money and time and interest into our future, our children.

—RICH RUFFALO, *New Jersey Teacher of the Year*

My greatest hope as a teacher is that, through my example, children, parents, teachers, and everyone with whom I have contact will learn how to interact with children and each other with mutual respect, integrity, and love. The children in my charge become a community of respect, integrity, love, acceptance, and belonging.

> —MICHAEL STIGLETS,
> *Forest Park, Oklahoma, Teacher of the Year*

Everyone must be accountable for the public education system. That's why it's called the public education system.

> —*Georgia's* ANDY BAUMGARTNER,
> *National Teacher of the Year*

To Be the Best

Teaching is as interesting as teachers make it.

—BECKY GOODWIN, *Kansas Teacher of the Year*

In our classroom, we have an additional three R's: respect, responsibility, and restraint. That's what life is.

—MARJORIE WEST, *Colorado Teacher of the Year*

I try to always hold onto my "Three Fs" of middle-school teaching: Be firm, be funny, and—most of all—be fair.

—*Alaska's* CYNTHIA PETROVICH,
BP Teacher of Excellence

My essential guidelines for the teaching profession can be summarized with four words: Connect, Care, Create, and Challenge.

—SUSAN BENJAMIN,
New Mexico Teacher of the Year

Good teachers possess common traits. They have a constant hunger for knowledge and a genuine desire to share that which they have learned. Bringing to the classroom an unlimited supply of energy and enthusiasm, their very presence invites students to follow them on a journey to discover things new and exciting. As if by magic, their enthusiasm becomes contagious.

—*Tennessee's* TERRY WEEKS,
National Teacher of the Year

No child leaves my room without a strong understanding of the curriculum or the words "respect" and "perseverance."

—PATTI A. DONNELLY, *Chapel Hill–Carrboro,
North Carolina, Teacher of the Year*

I have two rules. First, I have a right to teach and no one is going to interfere with that. And second, everyone has a right to learn and no one is going to interfere with that, either.

—CHAD GILLILAND,
Richardson, Texas, Secondary Teacher of the Year

There are at least three essential elements common to all excellent teachers: a deep concern and honest compassion for students; a knowledge and love of the subject matter; and a visible demonstration of energy, enthusiasm, and creativity in teaching methods.

—*Florida's* TRACEY L. BAILEY,
National Teacher of the Year

I have five fundamental beliefs which guide my teaching: accept all students where they are; never make it easy for students to fail; never give up on a student because he fails to learn; teach students to think; and, provide opportunities for students to develop beyond the classroom.

—*Virginia's* MARY V. BICOUVARIS,
National Teacher of the Year

Outstanding teaching starts with curiosity. Teachers who are curious experience the world in a different way.

—JESSE JOHNSON,
San Diego County, California,
Teacher of the Year

What comes through in my teaching is that I love my subject area a lot and want kids to love it as much as I do. The difference between play and learning is the kind of resolution a teacher brings to the activity. Not to see it as a game, but as a validation of a scientific principle.

—KATHERINE KOCH-LAVEEN,
Minnesota Teacher of the Year

School ought to be fun and interesting. You can learn a whole lot of information while you're having fun.

—AMY MONROE DENTY,
Georgia Teacher of the Year

All children like to laugh. Laughing with students is great fun and is not against the board of education's behavior code. More teachers should try it.

—LOIS LAPOINTE KIELY,
New Jersey Teacher of the Year

The teacher's kind disposition, aside from being a good educational tool, has an importance beyond the mere teaching of subject matter. The demonstration of love, understanding, and forgiveness is a human lesson profoundly vital to the education of each pupil in growth toward maturity and humanity.

> —*New York's* JAY SOMMER,
> *National Teacher of the Year*

To be a good teacher, you must give of yourself, share life experiences, make each student feel special, laugh, creatively relate subjects to real life, prove that there is a reason for learning, put a smile on a student's face, collaborate with colleagues, give extra time to a struggling student, have fun in the classroom, and more.

> —MARLA McCREA, *Chapel Hill–Carrboro,*
> *North Carolina, Teacher of the Year*

I'm able to do crazy things and inject humor into my lectures. I once told my students I always hated the marshmallow Peeps I used to get in my Easter basket as a kid, so they started bringing me the Peeps all week. So each day of the week leading up to Easter, I blew up Peeps using a different chemical reaction. I don't have many kids absent that week— they come for Peeps week, by golly!

> —BILL RICHEY, *Ohio Teacher of the Year*

Mine is not the most quiet and controlled classroom in the world. There is a lot of learning noise. There is a difference between noise and learning noise.

—LISA WOODS, *Conroe, Texas, Elementary School Teacher of the Year*

I keep the classroom a really happy place. I like to see the kids with smiles on their faces. I've even had kids say they want to stay here, after school has ended, because they're having fun. The classroom has to be fun for the kids, and if it's fun for them, it's fun for me, too.

—MARILYN MISA, *Teacher of the Year for the Catholic Diocese of Raleigh, North Carolina*

Teaching and life should be lived to the fullest, filled with learning and laughter and brimming with love for the world around you.

—RENEE GENBAUFFE O'LEARY, *Delaware Teacher of the Year*

Educators best promote students' intellectual maturation when we also foster in them that which cannot be readily measured and quantified:

emotional, spiritual, and cultural well-being; we do best by children when we predispose them to be happy and kind.

—W. CRAIG JOHNSON, *Chapel Hill–Carrboro, North Carolina, Teacher of the Year*

I'm known as a tough taskmaster, one who demands a lot from my students. Nevertheless, I've always let them know that I wouldn't demand anything of them that I wouldn't demand of myself. I also believe that we, as adults, should never promise these youngsters anything if we cannot deliver.

—SANDRA BROOKS DOBSON, *Washington, D.C., Teacher of the Year*

We have to set the example, we have to demonstrate to them that we are willing to help them in every way we possibly can. Our children watch us; they know everything we do. If you don't believe that, misplace something in your classroom.

—MAXINE BROWN, *Fayette County, Kentucky, Elementary School Teacher of the Year*

The research shows good teachers are good role models, who have a passion for teaching and they value the opinions of students. They work very hard at it, take risks, and are innovators. What they won't accept is failure in a student.

> —KATHERINE KOCH-LAVEEN,
> *Minnesota Teacher of the Year*

We have to stand up and, by our example, show that excellence can be attained.

> —RICH RUFFALO, *New Jersey Teacher of the Year*

I teach my students that the first step in making your dream into a reality is to put the idea on paper. Their idealism becomes activism. The activism yields results.

> —RONALD ADAMS,
> *Massachusetts Teacher of the Year*

If America is to remain strong and free we must do whatever it takes to give our youth an international perspective. We must teach our young people to respect the right of others to hold viewpoints different from their own, and to see the earth as mankind's home and a place where people share a common heritage. We must help our young people learn to be tolerant. As John Fitzgerald Kennedy said, "If we can't make the world safe for democracy, let's then make it safe for diversity."

—*Virginia's* MARY V. BICOUVARIS,
National Teacher of the Year

To expect students to know what they believe and who they are is to relate to them as persons of integrity and value.

—*Michigan's* THOMAS A. FLEMING,
National Teacher of the Year

Because we live in an entertaining society, kids want to be entertained. They have their Game Boy, the Internet. So for an educator, everything needs to be visual for them, and you have to use PowerPoint presentations, you have to include video, audio. You have to bring in real-life things into the classroom so they can relate and retain more. It's a lot of work to do that. You can't just give a lecture or hold up a book and ask questions. It will not work.

—HENRY BROWN III, *Florida Teacher of the Year*

Children need to be introduced to real-world issues to think about and be given opportunities to solve them. They need to believe that they can and should make a difference in their community and world. We need to teach about the world in personal ways with significant results. We must teach children the tools through which they can make the world more accessible, resourceful, friendlier, and stronger.

> —MARGARET HOLTSCHLAG,
> *Michigan Teacher of the Year*

My motto is, "If it isn't in their hands, it won't be in their brains."

> —ELIZABETH BUMGARNER, *Teacher of the Year at Tampa, Florida's Bay Crest Elementary*

As long as it isn't dangerous, I let them try it. Children must experience to learn.

> —BARBARA DORFF,
> *Texas Region X Secondary Teacher of the Year*

I create a safe, comfortable learning environment where students can relax and actively participate. I use lots of positive feedback and smiles to develop a sense of trust. I let them know I care.

> —SUSAN SHAW NILE, *Maine Elementary Level Physical Education Teacher of the Year*

Education is life. We learn as we live. Education shouldn't be separate from that. The more I can create a life feeling in my class, the better my kids can learn.

—MOLLY MERRY, *Colorado Teacher of the Year*

My classroom is student-centered. I have them do the teaching. I'm just there as a guide.

—MITSUYE CONOVER,
Oklahoma Teacher of the Year

You have to bring education to the student. You can't drag the student to the textbook because the textbook may not be where they are at.

—TIM BAILEY, *Utah Teacher of the Year*

If you just provide the kids with the skills they need and get out of their way, they'll do incredible things.

—ROBERT FOOR-HOGUE,
Maryland Teacher of the Year

A good teacher is always planning ahead. You don't see a good teacher rushing into the classroom on Monday morning scrambling for things to do. That teacher knows what's going to happen. By the same token that teacher is flexible enough to know that if what she has prepared does not work once she starts teaching, she should change course.

> —ANNIE PEGRAM,
> *North Carolina Teacher of the Year*

You need to absolutely know your subject very well and you need to really sell that subject. You can't be an excellent teacher without both of those.

> —BARBARA GORDON,
> *New York Teacher of the Year*

You have to love what you do. If you stand in front of kids and don't love it, they'll know.

> —KAY WILLIAMS,
> *Palm Beach County, Florida,*
> *Teacher of the Year*

I don't care if I'm known professionally as the neatest teacher in the hall, but hopefully as the teacher with the neatest ideas.

> —DEBBIE LACY,
> *Eldon, Missouri, Teacher of the Year*

Teachers constantly have to readjust. If you walk into my room you would see 100 things going on. It's growing up and learning in its true form.

—KATHERINE STAHL, *Indiana Teacher of the Year*

A lot of times we do not realize the magnitude of the impact we have. The little things we do can play a big part in influencing people. . . . We need to be aware in everything we do we are having an influence—be it a positive or negative one.

—CATHY BISSOONDIAL, *Illinois Teacher of the Year*

You have to get on the inside, give them some kind of motivation that makes them want to learn. It's an old pedagogy that says, "First you let the kids know who you are, then you let them try to find out who they are."

—DEBBIE ERWIN,
Hamilton County, Tennessee, Teacher of the Year

Most important in the teaching process is the relationship a teacher establishes with his pupils. A responsive, supportive relationship between teacher and student establishes the best kind of atmosphere for learning. Not persistent punitive measures, but kindness and understanding are the most potent forces in learning.

> —*New York's* JAY SOMMER,
> *National Teacher of the Year*

A good teacher knows that trust is everything and that children need to trust you because they put all of their faith in you. One instructor told me years ago, "Don't tell a child anything you cannot deliver because they will never let you forget it."

> —ANNIE PEGRAM,
> *North Carolina Teacher of the Year*

I keep it interesting for them so that it stays interesting for me. Nobody likes to do the same thing every single day. We manage to cover the required curriculum, but there's nothing that says you can't do that in an interesting way.

> —*Ohio's* SHARON M. DRAPER,
> *National Teacher of the Year*

Many adults would rather be fishing or playing golf than working, so managers try to find ways to motivate them. It's the same with students. I look for ways to motivate kids.

—CHRIS SHORE, *Riverside County, California, Mathematics Teacher of the Year*

You have to compete with "Sesame Street" and "Barney" and everything else. You have to be an actress on a stage sometimes to get their attention and motivate them.

—SISTER JUDY DEWIG, *Germantown, Tennessee, Teacher of the Year*

Never give up. You try everything you can and when that doesn't work, you find more. As a teacher you have only 180 days with them. It's important that you do your part to prepare them for the next level.

—TERRI K. FISHBOUGH, *Tulare County, California, Teacher of the Year*

Teachers have to become good public relations experts. We have to be advocates for ourselves. No longer can we close the door to our classrooms and do a good job in the classroom and say that we're confident that we're doing a good job and that our kids are getting a good education. We have to go out and tell that story to the American people so they can understand what really is happening in our schools.

> —*Virginia's* PHILIP BIGLER,
> *National Teacher of the Year*

It's true when they say that to be a teacher, you have to wear many different hats. You're a nurse and a guidance counselor, and a parent and a grandparent, and a friend.

> —DEBORAH WHEELER, *Teacher of the Year at*
> *Virginia's Mount Vernon Elementary*

The best days are when half the class agrees on one answer and the other half agrees on another. This leads to some great discussion.

> —GEORGE WATSON, *Delaware Teacher of the Year*

A kid can memorize anything he wants. But . . . a kid is going to remember how they were taught a lot more than what they were taught.

> —MIKE BYNUM, *Oklahoma Teacher of the Year*

The most important advice that I can give to any teacher is that they must always look for and celebrate their successes, no matter how small or sparse. Ours is not a profession that provides a great deal of validation or gratitude but it can provide a wealth of gratification. I would encourage every teacher to remember that in many cases we are the most influential adults in our students' lives and, as such, must be strong advocates for the rights and well-being of all children.

> —*Georgia's* ANDY BAUMGARTNER,
> *National Teacher of the Year*

There are lots of teaching strategies, but loving what you teach is essential. Believe in what you teach, live what you teach.

> —JACK DENTON,
> *Hamilton County, Tennessee, Teacher of the Year*

Passing the
Teaching Torch

...her because of teachers. They showed me
...someone other than my mother could love me.

—*Minnesota's* GUY R. DOUD,
National Teacher of the Year

When I see a young person who has a burning love
for learning, a passion for new ideas and life in
general, a desire to help others, and thrives on
challenges, I know I am in the presence of a
potential teacher. I would recommend that this
young person enter the teaching profession, because
only in teaching can we satisfy all of these ideals.

—*California's* MARILYN JACHETTI WHIRRY,
National Teacher of the Year

My most capable students who would express a
desire to teach would hear from me words of
encouragement, not promises of glory, money, or
open gratitude.

—*Virginia's* MARY V. BICOUVARIS,
National Teacher of the Year

Encourage exceptional young people to enter the
teaching profession. We readily assume that these

talented students should pursue law or medicine. Certainly, those are wonderful options, but we also must include teaching among their choices. The message is powerful: "You would be a wonderful teacher. Please consider using your talents on behalf of children." If each of us says this to just one student—and means it—then we soon will transform the way the teaching profession is perceived.

—CHRISTA M. COMPTON,
South Carolina Teacher of the Year

My dream to become a professional educator was because of my wonderful childhood school experience, the brilliant and nurturing teachers in my past and present, and the support and care given by my parents, family, and friends.

—CHARLES MERCER JR.,
Washington, D.C.,
Teacher of the Year

My life has been filled with role models who were educators. It was no wonder that I always planned on becoming a teacher. As a member of the teaching profession, my respected colleagues have all inspired

me to become the best I can be, and have all
contributed to any success I have had.

> —TANYA N. MARCINKEWICZ,
>   *Delaware Teacher of the Year*

I was able to make it because I had teachers who
believed in me. And I had parents that said, "There's
no such thing as an excuse. Sorry about your luck,
you grew up in the projects, but get over it." So life
isn't fair, we deal with what we have. We can go,
"Poor pitiful me," or we can say, "I'm going to deal
with it, I'm going to take advantage of every
opportunity life gives me."

> —TINA STEVENSON,
>   *Fayette County, Kentucky,*
>   *Middle School Teacher of the Year*

I never thought I wanted to be a teacher, but when I
look back, I realize the seed was in me. When I was
7, 8, and 9 years old, I played school on the front
porch. I remember sitting the kids in rows on the
steps, giving them questions I always knew the
answers to. If they got the right answer, they got to
move up a step, like going to the next grade. . . . I
really enjoy the classroom, the interaction between

students and staff. It has become such a part of me, that joy of discovery and wonder.

> —DONNA GRAHAM,
> *Washington, D.C., Teacher of the Year*

There is nothing I like more than when one of my students says, "Can you give me a recommendation? I want to get a degree in education."

> —FRANCISCO MARMOLEJO,
> *Orange County, Florida,*
> *Community College Teacher of the Year*

Teaching is not for the faint-hearted, the indecisive, the timid, the believer in the status quo, or the one who is just seeking a job, not a profession. Teaching is for those who really want to teach and place the academic climate of their students above their own personal desires. Teaching results when the teacher is a facilitator, a seeker of incentives, and a motivator.

> —HELEN CASE,
> *Kansas Teacher of the Year*

I recommend teaching to someone who feels excited about the possibility of influencing the development of young minds, and doesn't mind hard work, both physical and mental.

> —*Michigan's* THOMAS A. FLEMING,
>   *National Teacher of the Year*

We have to talk about the positive aspects of teaching, the lives you can change and the difference you can make. We have to talk more about that and less about the problems. There are problems that need to be changed, so I'm not saying we should cover them up, but we need to focus on the purpose of teaching and sell that dream to more people, because that's what really makes a good teacher: when she or he really believes that they can impact children.

> —MARY MORELAND,
>   *Muscogee County, Ohio, Teacher of the Year*

The stereotype was that teachers had to be motherly women, maternal. I had to show that I could be paternal, which is just as good or better since many of these kids don't have fathers at home. Little boys in school need to see men succeeding.

> —*Georgia's* ANDY BAUMGARTNER,
>   *National Teacher of the Year*

If you have any interest in becoming a parent and you love children, you can't find a better occupation. The children can come to school with you, they are off when you're off, and it creates such a wonderful atmosphere when you have a relationship with your child even during the workday.

—JUDITH SOLOVEY,
Hamilton County, Tennessee, Teacher of the Year

My being a male in the nontraditional role of nurturing, patient teacher has caused many daddies and grandpas to realize that one can still be a man if he plays Barbie or tea party, and one's masculinity is not jeopardized when he drops to his knees in order to be at eye level with the child who is talking to him.

—MICHAEL STIGLETS,
Forest Park, Oklahoma, Teacher of the Year

I worry about the future of education as our veteran teachers retire. We must cultivate the dignity and emphasize the societal worth of the individual teacher and of the teaching profession.

—BARBARA GORDON,
New York Teacher of the Year

I was that very shy child who was so afraid to take a risk and do anything. My first-grade teacher made me feel at home, and I knew from that day on that I wanted to be a teacher and I never changed my mind. I thought, "If I can do for them what she did for me . . ."

—MELANIE MARTIN,
   Richardson, Texas,
   Elementary Teacher of the Year

The biggest paradox is when a student tells me that her dad told her, "Don't go into teaching because the money is bad." I tell her to go ask him if he wants her to have good teachers.

—BILL RICHEY, *Ohio Teacher of the Year*

It's not that they doubted my ability to be a good teacher, but they couldn't match my profile to their notion of the kind of person who becomes a teacher. Surely I would want to make money, pursue a law degree, or consider business school. I would only look quizzically at these naysayers and ask, "Who exactly should be in the classroom? People with no other options?" This is a vocation for those with keen minds, compassionate hearts, boundless energy, and unlimited patience. I am proud that it is my calling.

—Christa M. Compton,
South Carolina Teacher of the Year,
on those who told her not to become an educator

We've come a long way from the old adage, "If you can't do, you teach." That is an old adage I always felt was lacking because I could name off any number of people that could be successful at anything and they chose to be teachers.

—Frank D. Gawle,
Connecticut Teacher of the Year

We must educate people to understand that what we do is highly skilled, deeply meaningful, and can be very rewarding, complex work. The assumption that anyone can teach is not true. We must disabuse people of that notion.

—*Vermont's* Michele Forman,
National Teacher of the Year

It is imperative that we raise the prestige of the profession. That means that teachers need to be treated as professionals and to be seen as uniquely skilled individuals. Not everybody has the ability to teach. I have seen high-profile and very wealthy lawyers turn to Jell-O in front of a group of 15-year-olds.

>—*Virginia's* PHILIP BIGLER,
>   *National Teacher of the Year*

When I was in high school, the one thing I was sure of was that I was never going to be a teacher. At the age of 40, that's when I decided I wanted to get real . . . When I got into teaching, it was the first time that I felt like I had a career.

>—LINDA ADAMSON, *Maryland Teacher of the Year*

When you are in your classroom you have constraints to work within, but within those constraints you have many decisions to make. To a very large degree, teachers are their own bosses.

>—DOUGLAS W. COOPER, *Ohio Teacher of the Year*

The world will tell you to play it safe, but I say play it all. The world will tell you to make money. I implore you to make friends and to make a difference.

—CHRISTA M. COMPTON,
  South Carolina Teacher of the Year

At each and every low point in my life, there has been a teacher that reached out her hand to me. It seems there was also a teacher present to share the triumphs in my life, offering a hug, a note of recognition, or just a simple smile. It has been through the kindness and love of teachers in my life that I found the inspiration to pursue this noble profession. I owe a debt to teaching I don't know I can repay.

—REBECCA CURRY,
  Camden County, Florida, Teacher of the Year

INDEX